Contents

Consumption

KEY CONCEPTS

Published

Consumption

Alan Aldridge

polity

First published in 2003 by Polity Press in association with Blackwell
Publishing Ltd

Reprinted 2004, 2005, 2008, 2009

Polity Press
65 Bridge Street
Cambridge CB2 1UR, UK

Polity Press
350 Main Street
Malden, MA 02148, USA

ISBN: 978-0-7456-2529-4
ISBN: 978-0-7456-2530-0 (pb)

A catalogue record for this book is available from the British Library and
has been applied for from the Library of Congress.

Typeset in 10.5 on 12 pt Sabon
by SNP Best-set Typesetter Ltd., Hong Kong
Printed and bound in the United States by Odyssey Press Inc.,
Gonic, New Hampshire

For further information on Polity, visit our website: www.polity.co.uk

For Meryl Aldridge

Acknowledgements

I should like to begin by thanking the staff and postgraduate students in the School of Sociology and Social Policy at the University of Nottingham for their interest in and support of my work on this book. The staff at Polity Press have been extremely efficient, friendly and supportive; it has been good to work with them. There are a number of colleagues I should particularly like to thank for their generosity. Gerry Hanlon had the delightful and increasingly rare habit of wandering into my room to discuss the sociology of consumption rather than the latest imperious demands from the UK's regulators of Higher Education. José López provided penetrating theoretical comments that helped me to get some important concepts far clearer. Nick Stevenson made a number of crucial observations which both set me thinking and encouraged me to keep at it. Tim Strangleman has been an unfailing source of original ideas, books to read, and comradely support. Our cat Dido regularly reminded me that production does not take priority over consumption. Above all, I should like to thank Meryl Aldridge for just about everything, including decisive sociological comments on key issues that I and everyone else had overlooked.

1

Consumption as a Key Concept

Given the flourishing literature on the subject, we might simply take it for granted that consumption is a 'key concept' in the social sciences. But what is a key concept, and does consumption deserve that status?

The metaphor of a 'key' suggests a number of features. A key unlocks the way to another place, enabling us to explore new domains. A key in music is a tonal system that structures our perceptions and organizes our experience. A key is a solution to a puzzle, mystery or code; with it, we can decipher the meaning of people's words and acts.

This metaphor may obscure the fact that key concepts are contested. People disagree profoundly about their definition and significance. On reflection this is hardly surprising, given that reality is defined through concepts. George Orwell's novel, *1984*, offers an arresting demonstration. A language, 'Newspeak', is constructed to impose meanings by systematically impoverishing the English vocabulary. It does so in two main ways. First, the sense of words is brazenly inverted: the Ministry of Peace wages war, the Ministry of Truth spreads propaganda, the Ministry of Plenty enforces rationing and the Ministry of Love tortures dissidents. Second, all the nuanced evaluative words in the English language are reduced to a stark contrast between 'good' and 'bad'. Even that is too rich for the authorities, who cleverly replace 'bad' by 'ungood'. The citizens of Oceania are left with a sixfold scale on which their feelings are quantified: doubleplusgood – plusgood – good – ungood – plusungood – doubleplusungood. The scale lacks a middle term, preventing people from taking up a neutral position. It is, as a character in the novel smugly explains, really only one word. When Newspeak becomes universal, 'thoughtcrime' will be impossible.

Newspeak requires the suppression of history and memory. As each new edition of the Dictionary is published the previous version is destroyed, erasing what little linguistic variety had survived. As with any key concept, to understand the contemporary meanings of consumption we need to recover its history – an essential part of Raymond Williams's project in his illuminating book *Keywords* (1976).

The word 'consume' dates from the fourteenth century. Its original meaning was pejorative: to use up, destroy, devour, waste, squander, exhaust. 'Consumer' dates from the sixteenth century, with similar pejorative connotations. 'Consumption' originally referred to any wasting disease, before becoming the (now old-fashioned) term for severe pulmonary tuberculosis.

From the mid-nineteenth century, Williams points out, 'consumer' mutated into a neutral term in bourgeois political economy. Increasingly what was spoken of was '*the* consumer', an abstract entity in opposition to 'producer', just as 'consumption' stood in contrast to 'production'. This neutral, abstract usage passed into general use in the mid-twentieth century, and has since become dominant.

The ascendancy of the abstract bourgeois consumer, Williams argues, imposes an ideology that flattens out meaning. Older terms slowly decline. 'Customer', which from the mid-fifteenth century implied a continuing personal relationship with a supplier, was gradually replaced by 'consumer', an abstract figure in an impersonal market. Customers have needs which they have freely chosen, and these needs are met by suppliers. Consumers have needs that are created by people who then purport to satisfy them. Unlike the customer, the consumer inhabits a world saturated with advertising. Once no more than information tricked out with puff, advertising becomes an insidious mechanism for the creation of need. Ironically, there is much talk of 'consumer choice' – for Williams, a self-contradiction.

'Consumer' and 'consumption', he argues, have become the dominant terms through which we conceptualize our relationship to all manner of goods and services. Relevant distinctions are in danger of being lost. He points to the irony of so-called consumer organizations, whose aim is to act both as pressure group and as source of information for people seeking quality and value. How revealing, Williams suggests, that discriminating purchasers should be referred to as their opposite: consumers. My own work has made a similar point, though at the time I was not aware that Williams had been there before me: the Consumers' Association, I wrote (A. Aldridge 1997: 406), 'has succeeded in delivering commodified information to individual consumers, but failed to create an informed public'.

The pejorative meanings associated with consumption, consumerism and 'the' consumer are ammunition for cultural critics. Many examples will be discussed throughout this book. Consider just one: Bauman's exposition of what he calls 'the consumer attitude' (Bauman 1990: 204, cited by Lury 1996: 50). What does it mean, Bauman asks, to have and to display a consumer attitude? He identifies five elements:

'It means, first, perceiving life as a series of problems, which can be specified, more or less clearly defined, singled out and dealt with.' Ours is a life of decisions rather than of chance, destiny or drift. We are required to manage our life as if we were running a small business. I would add that if we are very successful we might become a celebrity, in which case we shall be running not a small business but a modern corporation.

'It means, secondly, believing that dealing with such problems, solving them, is one's duty, which one cannot neglect without incurring guilt or shame.' This is Puritanism in modern dress. We are expected to treat consumption as work, and to perform it as a duty to society and to ourselves. Vocations from God may have declined, but society calls – and is even more demanding than the Almighty.

'It means, thirdly, trusting that for every problem, already known or as may still arise in the future, there is a solution – a special object or recipe, prepared by specialists, by people with superior know-how, and one's task is to find it.' Two cultural elements are combined here. One is optimism: no problem lacks a solution. From this stems the managerialist cant that there are no problems, only 'opportunities'. Consumerism, as we shall see, pervades the world of work. The other element is faith in expertise. Consumerism and professionalism form a paradoxical but deep alliance: the sovereign consumer needs constant professional advice.

'It means, fourthly, assuming that such objects or recipes are essentially available; they may be obtained in exchange for money, and shopping is the way of obtaining them.' Here is the recurrent theme of commodification of culture. Solutions are packaged and sold to us. Bocock's bitter comment captures the essence of the critique of commodification: for him consumerism is 'the active ideology that the meaning of life is to be found in buying things and pre-packaged experiences' (Bocock 1993: 50). Problems are manufactured precisely in order to sell solutions.

'It means, fifthly, translating the task of learning the art of living as the effort to acquire the skill of finding such objects and recipes, and gaining the power to possess them once found: shopping skills and purchasing power.' The consumer attitude is part of our very being, creating the very anxieties that it claims to allay. This is how we live our spiritually impoverished lives. We do not just consume, we have become consumers.

One theme picked out in Bauman's second point is the legacy of Puritanism, at least in Protestant cultures. The British suspicion of extravagance – an attitude that until recently encouraged a drab rejection of 'fashionable clothing, jewellery, eating and drinking well at home and restaurants' (Bocock 1993: 12) – can be traced back to the sixteenth-century Reformation and to Cromwell's government in the seventeenth. Bocock points the contrast with the more relaxed, guiltlessly self-indulgent cultures of Catholic France, Spain and Italy.

Exactly the same argument is made about the USA by Scitovsky in *The Joyless Economy* (1976). According to him, American consumerism carries the deadening impress of Puritanism. People who 'graze' throughout the day deny themselves the pleasures of a regular cycle of mealtimes;

technological innovation, the rush of fashion, and planned obsolescence mean that energy is drained into expenditure on and maintenance of consumer goods; over-reliance on the automobile deprives consumers of the pleasure of walks in the open air; central heating and air conditioning produce a sterile controlled environment inside buildings; and life's minor troubles are turned into occasions for medical and psychiatric intervention.

Bauman is not alone in stressing the profound anxieties, ambivalence and contradictions of consumerism. Miles (1998), for example, writes of the 'consuming paradox'. Consumption is experienced as both enabling and constraining. Despite the multitude of opportunities apparently available, we are severely limited in the choices open to us. Commercialization and commodification attract and repel, satisfy and alienate. One telling example is the commercialization of association football in England and other rich countries (Miles 1998: 136–40). Football teams are multi-million pound merchandizing corporations with brand names to protect and nourish. Television plays a dominant role in commodifying football for the fans. Supporting a premier league team is far more comfortable than standing on the bleak terraces once was, and the football is more athletic and skilful; but these seductions are bought at the cost of alienation, exploitation and financial exclusion.

Edwards (2000) similarly writes of the 'contradictions' of consumption. Consumers enjoy power but are also constrained; consumption is enjoyable and frustrating; people are embraced by the world of consumption and excluded from it; consumption is essential to free market capitalism but also corrosive of it.

Consumption is not merely contested, it is – like 'power' in Lukes's influential analysis – an *essentially* contested concept (Lukes 1974). Consumption is, moreover, a member of a family of essentially contested concepts including 'the' consumer, consumer society, consumer culture, and consumerism. It is in the nature of such concepts that no agreement about their definition will ever be achieved; the contest is interminable. We cannot all agree on a definition, because to do so would inevitably mean a victory for some of us and a defeat for others. Take, for example, the definition of consumerism. Definitions are endless, but can be grouped into three broad categories.

First, consumerism may be defined as a *social movement*, referring to pressure groups that test goods and services, recommend best buys and campaign for consumer rights. This is the definition commonly adopted in textbooks in economics and business studies, for example Loudon and Della Bitta's *Consumer Behavior* (1993: 627): 'Consumerism is a social movement of citizens and government to enhance the rights and powers of buyers in relation to sellers.' Here citizens are equated with consumers, and consumers are equated with buyers. Consumerism is presented favourably: it is about the empowerment of consumers as citizens, upholding their rights, protecting them from abuses of power, and supplying them with objective information that will help them to make rational choices. All this is held to contribute to the efficient working of a healthy market economy.

Second, consumerism may be defined as a *way of life*. It often implies, as many authors have noted, an excessive, even pathological preoccupation with consumption – 'lifestyles geared to possession and acquisition', in Lyon's words (1994: 67). Writers who, like Fiske (1989), emphasize the pleasures of consumption are attacked for providing an uncritical celebration of consumption that ignores the operation of power in capitalist society.

Third, consumerism may be defined as an *ideology*. Its purpose is to legitimize capitalist societies, contrasting them favourably with such alternatives as communism, fascism, and neofeudal despotisms, none of which come anywhere near satisfying the needs and legitimate expectations of ordinary people for comfort and prosperity.

Whatever definitions are adopted, important issues are at stake. The literature on consumption is a battlefield for competing visions of the good life. Key features of these battles are the following:

Consumption is a value-loaded concept

Essentially contested concepts are not value neutral, which is one reason why they are contested. They are a moral battleground for competing values and ideologies. As we shall see in chapter 3, the vision of the free market as the good society in operation is supported by its claim to deliver a wealth of goods and services to free and rational consumers who know what they want. Conversely, we can see the dark side of consumption in the pejorative meanings associated with consumerism, such as materialism, opportunism, selfishness, hedonism, and narcissism.

Consumption is typically seen in opposition to other concepts

Consumption does not stand in isolation. As with all key concepts there is an implied other. Among the most common oppositions are:

consumption – production;
consumption – investment;
consumption – citizenship;
consumption – conservation.

In each case there is usually a latent implication that consumption is inferior to its opposite: parasitic consumers versus useful producers, profligate consumers versus prudent investors, passive consumers versus active citizens, and selfish consumers versus responsible conservationists.

Consumption is a focus of dispute between academic disciplines

The literature on consumption is polarized into two camps, in accordance with a strict academic division of labour between, as Slater (1997: 51) puts it, 'the study of formally rational behaviour (economics) and the study of its irrational, cultural content (the rest)'. Sociologists, cultural theorists and social and cultural anthropologists are in the vanguard of attacks on economic models of consumption, 'the' market and 'the' consumer – attacks which economists serenely ignore.

The war between economics and its detractors is not the only contest. Sociology has been regularly criticized by social anthropologists for its sweeping generalizations unsupported by serious ethnography. According to their account, sociologists are often little better than economists, since they both peddle stereotypes of 'the' consumer. Similarly, cultural studies has often involved a critique of sociological writing. Cultural studies has been seen to offer imaginative and fine-grained accounts of consumption that are attuned to the rich aesthetics of contemporary lifestyles, and that have broken free from sociology's apparent obsession with social class and production.

Consumption is integral to images of the good society and its opposite, dystopia

Utopian writing typically envisages a fundamental reordering of the relationship between production and consumption. Some utopias are societies of abundance, others abstain from material gratifications in pursuit of higher ideals. A typical utopian move is to abolish money, promising to reward us according to our needs or our merits. Most, perhaps all, utopias can just as plausibly be seen as dystopias. This is the subject of chapter 3.

Consumption is bound up with notions of what it is to be a fully developed human being morally and spiritually

According to an influential theory put forward by Abraham Maslow (1970), human motivation across all societies and at all times is organized in a hierarchical structure of need. As each lower level of need is met, so the next higher level comes into force. Maslow's 'need hierarchy' has seven levels, which in descending order are:

Self-actualization needs;
Aesthetic needs;
Cognitive needs;
Esteem needs;

Belongingness and love needs;
Safety needs;
Physiological needs.

One way to read Maslow's need hierarchy is as a ladder on which we climb from brutishness to humanity. And one way of stating the limitations of consumer society is to say that it can satisfy only our animal needs. Consumerism can meet our physiological need for nutrition and our safety need for shelter. By the time we reach the third and fourth levels – belongingness, love and esteem – consumerism, like Mephistopheles, delivers the semblance but not the substance. We may try to purchase love, friendship and respect, but what we buy will be prostitutes, parasites and toadies. At levels five and six – our cognitive need for knowledge and understanding and our aesthetic need for beauty – consumerism is a spent force. As for self-actualization, the fulfilment of our potential as human beings, consumerism is its antithesis. Consumerism does not raise us up, it drags us down.

Another strand in thinking about consumerism and what it is to be human derives from the ethical writings of Aristotle. His influence runs powerfully through MacIntyre's (1985) analysis of the poverty of contemporary moral philosophy, and Sennett's (1998) discussion of the processes by which character has been corroded by changes in the world of work. In his contribution to a collection of essays on the good life, Scruton (1998) argues in Aristotelian fashion that we must not confuse pleasure and happiness. Pleasure results from satisfying desires, but happiness comes through fulfilment as a person. Pleasure is precarious because it depends on good luck, but happiness is robust because it flows from virtue. Consumption delivers only pleasure, not happiness. But happiness, not pleasure, is the final goal of human life, and only virtuous people can be happy.

Stereotypes of the consumer

In figure 1.1 below (p. 16) I propose a classification of images of the consumer. This classification will be referred to throughout the book. It is offered, as I shall explain, as a tool with which we can analyse the issues at stake in debates about the meaning and significance of consumption as social movement, way of life, and ideology.

Debates about consumption and consumerism frequently revolve around stereotypes of the consumer. Consumers are treated as though they fitted neatly into one and only one stereotype. A useful list of these stereotypes has been provided by Gabriel and Lang (1995: 27–186), who identify nine different images of the consumer: as chooser, communicator, explorer, identity-seeker, hedonist/artist, victim, rebel, activist, or citizen.

The consumer as chooser

As rational actors, consumers are normally the best judges of their own interests. Hence they benefit from having the maximum possible choice, and access to objective information on which to base it. Consumer society brings more choice for the vast majority of people. The expression of choice through consumer demand is the driving force of economic efficiency, prosperity and growth. Choice is beneficial for social order, promoting the genuine social stability that only a free society can enjoy.

The consumer as communicator

In this portrait of the consumer, consumption is an activity through which people convey symbolic messages primarily to others but also to themselves. Material objects are not just useful items but carriers of meaning, typically serving as markers of social status. Veblen's (1925/1899) work on conspicuous consumption and Simmel's (1957/1904) discussion of fashion are pioneering texts on consumption as communication. Later theorists such as Douglas and Isherwood (1996) and Bourdieu (1984) built on the classics, replacing speculation with evidence and satire with analysis.

The consumer as explorer

Driven by insatiable curiosity, the explorer is on a quest for new experiences. A key activity for the consumer as explorer is bargain-hunting. This is not the same as demanding value for money. Instead, it involves taking advantage of anomalies in the market, and discovering hidden treasures such as the priceless Brueghel stacked unrecognized in someone's attic. Gabriel and Lang compare the bargain-hunter to the trickster, a mythological opportunist who uses guile and cunning to exploit the social system and other actors in it.

The consumer as identity-seeker

Arguably, we are less inclined than at any time in the past to think of identity as assigned at birth or conferred by society as a permanent status. Identity and status are achieved, not ascribed. The construction of identity is a lifelong self-aware project. Identity is fluid, potentially unstable and context-dependent – a key theme in postmodernist writing. Although this is often presented as liberation from fixed categories and assigned status, the struggle for identity is not necessarily benign. We crave wholeness and authenticity. Image can be purchased, and narratives can be made up; but what of respect and self-respect? Are we not concerned to distinguish between trustworthy and untrustworthy people, ourselves included? In Gabriel and Lang's account, the consumer as identity-seeker is presented as a forlorn and perpetually anxious figure.

The consumer as hedonist (pleasure-seeker)/artist

The emphasis here is on the pleasures of consumption. According to Campbell (1987, 1995), while traditional hedonism involved opulence, sumptuousness, and a multitude of voluptuous pleasures derived from the senses, modern hedonism seeks pleasure less in sensations themselves than in the emotions that accompany them. All emotions – including apparently negative ones such as sorrow, melancholy, and anger – can serve modern hedonism, if subject to appropriate self-control. Because it depends on emotional experiences rather than sensations, modern consumption stimulates imagination, dream and reverie. Life is aestheticized, and the consumer has therefore become a kind of artist. Traditional hedonists indulged themselves in the present; modern hedonists defer gratification in eager expectation of more intense pleasures in the future.

Daniel Bell (1979) argued that a cultural fault line runs through contemporary capitalism. Production requires discipline and hard work, whereas consumption generates the irresponsible pursuit of pleasure. On Campbell's analysis, however, there is no contradiction. Since hedonistic consumers continually seek new stimuli, their orientation is perfectly compatible with economic growth. Contrary to Bell, the spheres of production and consumption are driven by the same ethic. Consumption is a realm of seduction (Bauman 1990, 1998). What Bell identified as a contradiction in capitalism becomes in Bauman's hands a profitable symbiosis.

The consumer as victim

This theme, once a commonplace – Vance Packard's *The Hidden Persuaders* (1957) is a popular rendition of it, Marcuse's *One Dimensional Man* (1964) an intellectual version – has fallen from favour. Economists see the consumer as sovereign. Sociologists and anthropologists may repudiate 'sovereignty' as an ethnocentric ideological construct, but they still emphasize consumer agency. It has become a platitude to say that the consumer is not a 'dope' or a 'dupe' – but even so, smart people can still end up as victims. In some cases, intellectuals are more gullible than most, as shown by the sorry sight of Western thinkers lionizing Stalin at the height of his purges (Caute 1988). More prosaically, a conjuror who claims to bend spoons by psychic means has little to fear from an audience of physicists, whose faith in rationality means they can easily be deceived.

Consumer protection is widely recognized as necessary, and even free marketeers usually concede that consumers should be protected against fraud and deception. Some consumers may be particularly vulnerable, for example children, and people who are old, or sick, or infirm, or poor. Many writers have noted the gendered construction of victimhood: men are sovereign, women are victims. In some situations, typically where objective information is hard to get, most of us are easy targets for the swindlers (cowboy motor mechanics, corrupt financial advisers). Governments can gain political capital through protecting consumers, just as they can lose it if they fail to do so, as the crisis of 'mad cow disease' in Europe demonstrated.

The consumer as rebel

Rebellious consumers use mass-market products subversively and iconoclastically. They are guerrillas fighting against commodification. At the politically quiescent, fun-loving pole of rebellion, we find young people playfully distorting mass-market products – ripping their jeans, in Fiske's example (1989: 1–21) – as a stylistic expression of identity politics. At the radical pole, an angry revolt has erupted against transnational corporations as the vehicles of global capitalism. This is frequently allied with a commitment to alternative economic institutions, including self-provisioning, credit unions, and barter systems such as LETS (Local Exchange Trading Systems).

The consumer as activist

Consumer activism is expressed through pressure groups and social movements that declare themselves champions of the consumer cause. Gabriel and Lang distinguish four phases of consumer activism in the West: the co-operative movement, which embodied the principle of mutuality, vesting ownership in members, not shareholders; value-for-money consumer movements such as the Consumer Union in the USA and the Consumers' Association in the UK; politically engaged movements, such as Ralph Nader's, which promote the idea of consumer as citizen and attack giant corporations for their anti-consumer practices; and a morally charged alternative consumerism, including green, ethical, and fair trade consumerism. The inescapable tensions between these varieties of consumerism mean that they are seldom able to form a rainbow alliance.

The consumer as citizen

Is consumerism one way in which citizenship asserts itself, or are they incompatible? The claim that citizens have been *reduced to* consumers implies a loss of political engagement. Citizenship expresses a fundamental equality, while consumerism generates and feeds on inequality. Citizens have social, economic and political rights, but they also have duties and responsibilities; consumers have merely consumer rights, and the dubious 'protection' provided by regulators. Citizens engage in collective action to make society better, whereas consumers are preoccupied with improving their own individual lot. Citizens move in the public domain, consumers retreat into a private refuge. On such accounts, citizenship is not an aspect of consumerism but its antithesis.

Against this is the argument that if people have rights as consumers of goods and services, it empowers them as citizens. Without consumer rights, citizens may be left at the mercy of private companies, public sector bureaucracies and powerful professions. While each of these may claim to be acting in the best interests of the people they 'serve', clients do not always find it so. Consumer organizations and consumer self-help groups have proved one of the most effective ways in which consumers can assert their rights as citizens.

So much for the details of Gabriel and Lang's list. Their underlying point is that 'the consumer' is a cultural fetish. Too often, in academic discourse and public debate, only one stereotyped image is held up as the true portrait of the consumer. Alternatively, the nine images are presented as mutually exclusive, excluding consideration of the complex ways in which they can be combined.

One reason for the prevalence of stereotypes of the consumer is the defence of disciplinary and ideological boundaries. The consumer as chooser is the property of neoclassical economics. Against this, rival disciplines, notably sociology and social anthropology, have emphasized other images, above all the consumer as communicator. Cultural studies has intervened in support of the consumer as hedonist/artist.

Academics are not the only interested parties. Pressure groups variously paint portraits of the consumer as chooser, or activist, or rebel. Organized consumerism, as I shall argue in chapter 6, is a project designed not simply to promote the interests of consumers but to create rational consumers, instructing us in what consumer organizations regard as the values, virtues and behaviours appropriate to rational consumption.

Our lived reality as consumers is not captured by the stereotypes. We often feel a welter of ambivalent and conflicting emotions. We can be irrational and rational, spontaneous and disciplined, individualistic and conformist, engaged and detached, knowing and innocent, bored and stimulated. Consumption can be a great liberation or a tedious chore. It may be a sphere of self-indulgent frivolity or moral engagement. We may be swept along or shut out. We may lose or find ourselves in it. And if we try to escape from consumption, where if anywhere shall we find the exit?

A classification of images of the consumer

Gabriel and Lang's catalogue of portraits falls short of being a classification or typology. First, the categories obviously overlap, as Edwards (2000: 11) points out. Activism and rebellion merge into each other, exploration is a subcategory of choosing, and identity-seeking is a form of communication turned inward on the self. Second, some of the types are underdeveloped, particularly the notion of consumer as explorer. Third, it is questionable whether the consumer as citizen is a face of consumerism at all. Citizenship, as Gabriel and Lang go on to argue (1995: 173–86), is not a variety of consumerism but a radical alternative to it. Fourth, the basis of the classification is unclear. What are the underlying criteria or dimensions? What are the relationships between the categories? Is the classification exhaustive, or are there other

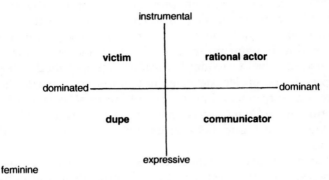

Figure 1.1   Images of the consumer in Western discourse

types that have been left out? Without answers to such questions, what we have is not a classification but simply a list.

I suggest that two fundamental issues underlie images of the consumer. The first is the question of power. Are consumers sovereign? Is it consumer demand that powers the market, forcing firms to respond by supplying people with the goods and services they want? Or are consumers' desires implanted in them by advertising, marketing, and the mass media – a manipulative apparatus of persuasion that seduces them into 'demanding' what the producers want to supply?

The second fundamental issue is this: what is consumption about? Is it primarily concerned with the instrumental purchase of goods and services for practical purposes – the car as a means of transport? Or is it a symbolic realm in which people exchange messages about class, status and identity – the car as status or sex symbol?

The horizontal axis in figure 1.1 represents the objective dimension of power, contrasting the powerful rational actors and communicators with the dominated victims and dupes. The vertical axis represents the subjective dimension of orientations to consumption, contrasting the instrumental rational actors and victims with the expressive communicators and dupes.

Since this classification will be referred to throughout the book, there are a number of crucial points to be clarified at the outset.

First, it is a classification of images of consumers, not of consumers themselves. It is concerned with the social construction of consumers in Western discourse about consumption. The classification is intended to help us to analyse that discourse and to examine what it tells us about the ways we construct our society and ourselves. An important aspect of this, as signalled in figure 1.1, is gender. The point is not that women are dupes while men are rational actors, but that much of Western discourse *constructs* consumption as gendered in this way.

Second, the underlying dimensions are more important than the classifications they generate. In the contrasts between rational actors, communicators, victims and dupes, the core issues are the distribution and exercise of power in society, and the nature of the human subject.

Third, the horizontal axis represents the dimension of power, not of rationality. Victims and dupes are not necessarily irrational, though the discourse may construct them so. Conversely, neither communicators nor even rational actors are necessarily rational. Attributions of rationality and irrationality are one way in which power manifests and legitimizes itself.

Fourth, although the vertical axis represents the dimension of subjective orientation to consumption, the opposition between instrumentality and expressiveness is a feature of discourse that may well stand in need of deconstruction. It is strikingly gendered. One might argue that a sign of a balanced personality and a healthy society is that the instrumental and the expressive are not driven apart but united.

Having established that the purpose of the classification is not to construct stereotypes but to analyse discourse, what follows are some preliminary comments about the four images of the consumer generated by the two dimensions.

The rational actor

The discipline of economics rests on the assumption that consumers behave rationally in pursuit of their self-interest.

'Economic man' is calculative and selfish; yet out of this seeming mediocrity arises the glory of free market capitalism, a society in which people are free, creative and prosperous. Adam Smith put it graphically:

> It is not from the benevolence of the butcher, the brewer, or the baker that we expect our dinner, but from their regard to their own interest. We address ourselves, not to their humanity but to their self-love, and never talk to them of our own necessities but of their advantages. Nobody but a beggar chooses to depend chiefly upon the benevolence of his fellow-citizens. Even a beggar does not depend on it entirely. (1970/1776: 119)

Benevolence is a virtue, as Smith himself insists. The point, however, is that society runs on self-interest, not altruism.

Although the economist's rational choice approach focuses on the consumer as rational actor, it can deal reasonably comfortably with two of the remaining three types. First, it can recognize victims. People do make poor choices, sometimes because they behave irrationally, sometimes because they lack objective information, and sometimes because they have been swindled. Hence the need for consumer protection. Hence too the role of consumer organizations, campaigning for consumer rights and supplying impartial assessments of goods and services. Advocates of the free market usually recognize a place for consumer protection, though they tend to warn against 'the nanny state'. *Caveat emptor* – let the buyer beware – is a treasured axiom. Their remedy for victimhood is more freedom, not less.

Second, the rational choice approach can easily embrace the consumer as communicator. Take for example the case of luxury goods. Contrary to what is sometimes thought, luxuries are not a problem for rational choice theory. Cultural critics may well see the purchase of Parisian perfume as foolish extravagance, since equally good alternatives are available far more cheaply, including soap. Economists do not take this view. Snob value is still value, so cheap substitutes are not 'equally good'. The dance of seduction involves symbolism and imagination, and scent from Paris can enhance its wearer's allure. Similarly, young people who buy fashionable branded sportswear at premium prices because they give them status among their peers are not mistaken. It is consumers, not critics, who are living in the real world.

The rational choice approach is resistant to the notion that consumers are dupes. Such talk is seen as no more than condescension by intellectuals towards people they take to be their cultural inferiors. 'Taste', as Bourdieu (1984) argued, is an expression of symbolic power.

The communicator

Four of Gabriel and Lang's nine images of the consumer – *communicator, identity-seeker, hedonist/artist* and *rebel* – are variants on the consumer as communicator. This focus on communication reflects the dominant concerns in sociology and cultural studies. It is a vivid illustration of what Campbell (1995) has called 'the communicative act paradigm'. Consumption is interpreted as the exchange of symbols between actors who are trying to convey to one another messages about their lifestyle and identity. Instrumentality is denied: we never buy things simply because they are useful. It is impossible, on this view, to consume without communicating. Anti-consumerism cannot avoid being a style of consumption.

The communicative act paradigm involves, I suggest (A. Aldridge 1998: 2), an *over-culturalized* concept of humanity. On occasions we should treat a washing machine less as a symbol than as a machine for washing clothes (Goldthorpe et al. 1969: 184n).

The victim

Victims have been neglected in the literature on consumption. Little interest has been shown in these failed rational actors, yet consumer society offers limitless opportunities to be victimized. Consumers may unwittingly purchase forgeries or stolen goods; they may succumb to chain letters, pyramid selling operations and similar get-rich-quick schemes; they may make unwise investments in ostrich farms or champagne; they may buy a car that was seriously damaged in a crash and has been repaired only superficially. More likely, at least in the UK, they have been missold financial products by reputable banks and insurance companies whose sales staff masquerade as financial advisers. At one time or another, most consumers will have made such mistakes, though they are often minor and can be simply absorbed as a lesson for the future.

Rational choice theory celebrates success rather than failure, and has a disposition to blame the victim, as in the principle of *caveat emptor*. On this view, victims are rightly condemned for their foolishness and should not be compensated for it. Blaming the victim is particularly plausible, at least to men, when the victim is a woman.

In contrast to economists, sociologists and cultural theorists have concentrated on the *communicator–dupe* axis, and on the critique of rationality. The rational actor is rejected as an artificial construct, and the victim is unfortunately thrown out with him.

The dupe

The most powerful and influential exposition of the consumer as dupe is to be found in the work of the Frankfurt School, discussed in chapter 3 (pp. 81–5). For the moment, we may illustrate the notion of the dupe by Finkelstein's analysis of the cultural practice of eating in restaurants.

Most people think of eating out as convenient and enjoyable. They are misguided, Finkelstein tells us. They may claim to experience it as pleasant and sociable, but the structural reality is artifice, control and surveillance.

Finkelstein robustly asserts the thesis of consumer as dupe. Consumers are easily manipulated by restaurateurs and waiters. People show so little insight into their own conduct that it is pointless to ask them about their opinion of dining out. Interviews and surveys will simply yield stock answers. Her aim in writing the book is to educate the reader by presenting arguments and insights 'in order to elicit a new vision of him/herself that opens up the possibility of personal reorientation' (Finkelstein 1989: 18). The goal is what Socrates called 'the examined life' – which according to him is the only life worth living. People are not, as writers such as Giddens (1991) believe, intensely reflexive. The examined life is rarely achieved, and consumerism cuts against it.

The problem with eating out, according to Finkelstein, is the commodification of experience. As an example, take the 'romantic' meal for two: the secluded corner table, candlelight, flowers, subdued music, the sunset over the harbour. All this is formulaic and scripted. We have purchased a sham. A stereotype has been packaged and cynically sold to us.

How could it be otherwise? Finkelstein's answer (1989: 177–8) is that eating out would be civilized if it were conducted without 'artifice', 'paraphernalia', 'hyperbole' or 'chicanery', and with the elimination of all 'ulterior' motives, including our own. What could be done about the restaurateur's ulterior motive of making a profit is not made clear.

For Finkelstein (1989: 8), a civilized appreciation of our companions can occur only 'in exchanges between individuals who are equally self-conscious and attentive to one another, who avoid power differentials and who do not mediate their exchanges through signatory examples of status and prestige'. This call for honesty without artifice is, as Mary Douglas (1973) has demonstrated, a typically 'Protestant' view. Ritual and symbolism are encumbrances to be swept away in order to arrive at pure authentic experience.

An evening out *à la* Finkelstein may be an authentic engagement with a fellow human being, though some might judge it a shade intense. In response to her despairing analysis, Warde and Martens suggest that people have good reasons to enjoy eating out. In Britain and elsewhere, it has become far less of an ordeal than it was in stuffier times. The intimidating rules of formal etiquette, a cause of embarrassment and derision, have disappeared from all but the most pretentious establishments. Restaurateurs are attuned to their clients' wish for companionship and conviviality. Warde and Martens conclude their book with this affirmation: 'In a world of geographic mobility, small households, smaller and unstable families, discontent with traditional divisions of labour, eating out is a rich source not of incivility, as Finkelstein maintained, but of conviviality and co-operation' (2000: 227).'

The classification set out in figure 1.1 recognizes the fact, as I have said, that Western discourse about the consumer is deeply gendered. At its most extreme, men are portrayed as autonomous and instrumental: 'economic man'. Women are constructed as dominated and expressive: 'fashion victims'. Men are rational actors, women are dupes.

In his analysis of lifestyles, Chaney (1996: 20–1) suggests that critics of consumerism tend to assume that women are susceptible to irrational persuasion and need protection from it. On this account, women and children are deliberately targeted by the advertising industry because they are so easily influenced. The contrast between men and women rests on two other oppositions: between producers and consumers, and between the public and the private spheres. Women's location in the private sphere of consumption is crystallized in the suburbs: 'Suburban housing', says Chaney, 'is the perfect physical form for the citizens of mass consumerism' (1996: 21). Chaney's argument is not that women are essentially dupes while men are essentially rational actors. Quite the reverse: these are not essences but social constructs.

Nowhere is the social construction of gender more evident than in discourse about shopping. Women are implicated in three ways: as shoppers, as shop assistants, and as shoplifters (Miller et al. 1998: 11–14). Shopping is typically dismissed as trivial. It is seen, not only in academic writing but in everyday talk, as a realm of self-indulgence, hedonism, individualism and materialism. We routinely equate shopping with excess, and use it as a symbol of the decadence of Western civilization. Shopping is a symbol through which we lament the spirit of our times.

Miller's (1998) ethnographic work shows how far the stereotype of shopping-as-indulgence strays from the lived reality of shopping as skilled action directed towards others, specifically to other members of the household. It is women's work; many men make poor companions on shopping expeditions, and when they go shopping by themselves for routine items their rationality deserts them. Women do 'treat' themselves during shopping, enjoying small indulgences as a reward for their hard work, but this concept of 'the treat' as an exceptional purchase points up thrift as the core activity

and paramount concern of shopping. Shopping is both more
banal and more important than culture critics recognize.

Three reasons to take consumption seriously

Although consumption is widely acknowledged to be a key
concept, many sociologists are uneasy at the seeming frivolity of some of the literature. Sport, television, fashion,
fandom, shopping, clubbing: these activities may be fun, but
are they not trivial distractions from the serious things in life
– work, politics, and maybe religion?

Perhaps the literature on consumption is an example of
what Rojek and Turner (2000) call 'decorative' sociology?
The term 'decorative' is an allusion to the work of the
Victorian political analyst, Walter Bagehot. He argued that
Britain's constitutional monarchy should be seen as belong-
ing to the decorative side of politics because it is divorced
from effective political decision-making. The monarchy is a
repository of national symbolism, and survives only because
it remains useful to politicians in their quest for legitimacy,
not because kings and queens wield power.

Decorative sociology, in Rojek and Turner's account,
ignores or misrepresents the operation of power in society,
and lacks any coherent concept of social structure. It therefore mistakes the aestheticization of life for the politicization
of culture. Identity politics replaces political reality, and
political correctness substitutes for political action.

Some writers on consumption are keen to distance themselves from the charge of decorative practice. That is why, for
example, Edwards (2000: 28–31) goes to some trouble to
assert his preference for the term 'consumer society' over
'consumer culture'. He does so to demonstrate that he is concerned not simply with aesthetics, but with the grounding of
consumption in its economic and political context.

To many critics, the communicative act paradigm (referred
to on p. 19 above) is a clear case of decorative sociology.
Lodziak (2002), for instance, is a trenchant critic of postmodern 'culturalist' theories of consumption that disregard
politics and economics in order to treat consumer culture as

a set of meaningful symbols imaginatively created by active consumers. The communicative act paradigm represents consumers as communicators operating skilfully in the expressive realm of symbolism. The focus is on spectacular displays of conspicuous consumption, rather than the everyday routine acts which, as Warde (2002: 19) reminds us, constitute most of our consumption practice. Buying bulk items such as petrol may seem unworthy of our attention as cultural theorists, until we remember the social, economic and political repercussions of the oil crisis of 1973–4. In the glorification of expressive consumption, dupes are not recognized – they are seen as the fictional creation of elitist critics who allow themselves to be scandalized by popular culture. Victims and rational actors are also excluded from the scene, because they are not thought to communicate anything (except perhaps frustration and resentment on the one hand, and self-satisfaction on the other).

What follows from the critique of decorative sociology is not that consumption fails as a key concept in the social sciences and should therefore be ignored, but that it is too important to be trivialized. I propose three reasons why consumption matters.

The good society: utopias and dystopias

Patterns of consumption are an integral part of conceptions of the good society and its opposite. In the contemporary world, the dominant utopian vision is that consumer paradise has been delivered by liberal democracy and free market capitalism. With victory over fascism and the implosion of communism, it has even been claimed that ideology and history have come to an end (Fukuyama 1992).

Critics argue that the fruits of free market capitalism are extreme inequality, conspicuous consumption, the erosion of community, the decay of civil society, rampant individualism, narcissism, and commodity fetishism. On these accounts, consumer society is not paradise but hell.

If we live in consumer society, we are bound to want to determine the accuracy of these rival accounts and to consider the likely consequences of acting on the basis of them.

The good life: pursuing pleasure or cultivating virtue?

Is consumer paradise the good life? Not according to much of the sociological literature, which paints a portrait of consumers as pathetically warped pleasure-seekers devoid of moral worth. At the opposite pole is the view that consumers are rational citizens pursuing their interests free from artificial restrictions and liberated from the internalized imperatives of the Protestant ethic. Between these two poles are more nuanced accounts which explore the multifaceted nature of consumer society as simultaneously liberating and oppressive, offering choice while also denying it, embracing some of us but excluding others.

Changing society: the role of culture

From 1979 to 1990, when Margaret Thatcher was Prime Minister, the UK experienced a huge social upheaval. It became obvious that Thatcherism was a programme of cultural as well as political and economic reconstruction. People would be freed from bondage to state bureaucracy, so that they could benefit from competition between private companies operating in a free market. Publicly owned assets would be transferred to the private sector, and everyone would be invited to reap the rewards of shareholder democracy. Dependency culture would be replaced by enterprise culture. The result would be freedom through self-reliance and mass affluence through the market.

Cultural reconstruction at the macro level was replicated at the micro level: managers of capitalist firms were spurred to embark on programmes of culture change, eradicating established working practices in pursuit of profit. Social institutions that stood in the way of reform – the professions, the education system, local government – were either transformed or abolished.

The triumph of Thatcherism caused disarray among the left. Thatcherism was a devastating hegemonic project, combining political and ideological strategies to gain popular consent. In Stuart Hall's words, written at the height of the Thatcherite era: ' It moulds people's conceptions as it restructures their lives as it shifts the disposition of forces to its side' (1988: 274–5). A crucial question for the left was, how to challenge Thatcherism's claim to have empowered the consumer?

For Hall and those associated with him, it was a claim that could not simply be dismissed. The left had to abandon its obsession with production and come to terms with consumer capitalism. The Puritan moralism of the left was offensive to most of its potential supporters (Stevenson 2002). Hall derided those on the left who liked the working class to be 'poor but pure' and 'unsullied by contact with the market' (1988: 213). The failures of state bureaucracies had to be faced, as did the market's potential to liberate people from dependency on the state and from deference to their social 'superiors'. Thatcherism was interpreted by Hall as 'authoritarian populism', a term which pointed not only to its inherent contradictions but also, equally significantly, to its grip on the popular imagination and its success in capturing people's dissatisfactions and aspirations. Mort put the challenge succinctly: 'the twin issues of consumerism and the market lie at the heart of the debate over our vision of the future of socialism' (1989: 160).

For First World societies, consumption is part of their vision of the good society, the good life, and the way to achieve them. It is hard to think that these subjects, which are addressed in the rest of this book, are merely decorative.

Consumption as a hidden key

Throughout the book we shall encounter widely diverging perspectives on consumption, consumerism and consumer society. The literature abounds with sharp contrasts and stark dichotomies. Consumption is set over against production, investment, citizenship and conservation. Dupes are contrasted with communicators, and communicators with rational actors (victims are usually forgotten). We appear to be faced with choosing between a bright but shallow optimism or a gloomy but deep pessimism; deep optimism appears to be self-contradictory. For most intellectuals there is little option: better to be gloomy than shallow. Hence cultural pessimism is the dominant mode in scholarly analyses of consumer society.

There is, as I said at the beginning of the chapter, a vast literature on consumption. Given the centrality of consumption to our visions of the good society and the good life, this abundance is scarcely surprising. What also needs to be observed, however, is that consumption plays a vital part in all manner of writing that appears at first sight to be about something else. It is always worth looking in the index of social science texts to see whether they contain any references to consumption, the consumer or consumerism. They frequently do. If we follow up these ostensibly stray and inconsequential leads, we are likely to find that, far from addressing consumption merely in passing, authors are grappling with the central issues we shall examine in this book. Consumption may be latent in these texts, but it is often crucial to comprehending what is at stake in debates about the good society and the good life.

Key concepts are even more influential when they are encoded and hidden from view.

2
Production and Consumption

From production to consumption?

Many critics have suggested that sociology has suffered from a 'productivist' bias. Their argument is that the system of production and the world of work have mistakenly been thought to determine patterns of consumption and the world of leisure. Even if this prioritizing of production over consumption was credible in the heyday of industrial capitalism, its validity today is increasingly called into question. Community has been eroded, social class is in decline, and work is no longer a central life interest for the vast majority of people. We are allegedly living in, or at least are rapidly moving towards, a society based on consumption.

For Zygmunt Bauman, the transition to consumer society has involved a series of displacements. I suggest the following are particularly important.

From the collective to the individual Unlike production, which necessarily involves collaboration, consumption is 'endemically and irredeemably lonely, even at such moments as it is conducted in company with others' (Bauman 2000: 165). The desires that consumption both stimulates and quenches are private sensations not easily communicated to others (Bauman 1998: 30). Consumption takes place in locations such as hypermarkets and shopping malls, which encourage action but not interaction, so that human encounters are brief and shallow. These places may be crowded, but there is no collectivity – a lonely crowd, in Riesman's evocative phrase.

Capital is freer from dependency on labour, but more dependent on consumers. National governments have to pursue economic deregulation to attract foreign investment. As consumers, people support deregulation. As workers, people know that disaster – short-time working, redundancy, unemployment – strikes at random. Collective defence is therefore pointless, and trade union membership and influence have declined as a result. The insecurity and uncertainty of contemporary societies are individualizing forces, as captured in Bourdieu et al., *The Weight of the World* (1999), where workers and union activists confront the collapse of the old certainties and the power base that sustained them.

From careers to portfolios of skills Few industries would now claim to offer 'a job for life'. A secure career, in which a worker moves predictably up a hierarchy, has been replaced by the notion of a portfolio of portable skills. Only the privileged few can sensibly embrace the ideal of work as a calling. Consumer goods are ideally fitted to the modern project of identity because they can so easily be obtained, consumed and discarded.

Unsurprisingly, trust in employers has faded. Bauman points out that 'Most rational people would prefer to entrust their life savings to the notoriously risk-ridden, stock-exchange-playing investment funds and insurance companies than to count on the pensions that the companies for which they work at present could provide' (2000: 166).

From savings to credit Deferred gratification, a pillar of the Protestant ethic, is no longer a virtue. Why put off enjoyment to an uncertain future that may never arrive? As Bauman remarks, 'A consumer society is a society of credit cards, not savings books' (1998: 31). The trouble that respectable working-class families used to take to conceal that they were buying goods on hire purchase is hard for later generations to comprehend.

From the work ethic to the aesthetics of consumption   Consumer society is regulated by aesthetics, not ethics. The call of duty has given way to a quest for pleasurable experiences. Only the fortunate few can find fulfilment in work as a vocation. Instead of planning for a long-term future, as the Protestant ethic demanded, consumers are alert to seizing opportunities as they arise.

Bauman argues that, compared to European societies, the USA was always less dependent on the work ethic. America drew instead on the spirit of enterprise and the desire for upward mobility, with work as a means to these ends, not an end in itself. The work ethic was not significant in Taylor's Scientific Management, which flourished at the beginning of the twentieth century and attracted the attention of the Bolsheviks in Russia, who saw it as a means to boost labour productivity. Scientific Management relied on money incentives to encourage workers to abandon their restrictive practices and work efficiently. The Taylorite worker was expected to seek freedom in and through consumption. Scientific Management appealed 'to the consumer hiding in the producer' (Bauman 1998: 22), an appeal which communism, with its productivist bias, failed to make.

From the modern to the postmodern self   The guiding principle of the modern self, as Elliott explains (2001: 144–51), is self-mastery. Operating in a rationalized world, the modern self is a project characterized by disciplined long-term planning to meet future goals. It is a project destined to perpetual dissatisfaction and disappointment, since neither the psyche nor society can be dominated by the human will. The modernist faith in self-mastery and social progress are both illusions.

The postmodern self lacks the solid foundations promised by modernism. Postmodern selves refuse to enter into long-term commitments, since loyalty is no longer a virtue but a foolish risk, and since the future is open and unpredictable. Cast adrift from the past and lacking confidence in the future, the postmodern self is fixated on the here-and-now.

For Bauman (2001: 14), 'The history of consumerism is the story of breaking down and discarding the successive tough and "solid" obstacles which limited the free flight of fantasy, and in Freud's vocabulary trimmed the "pleasure principle" down to the size dictated by the "reality principle".' In a consumer society, the concept of 'need' is rendered problematic. The once solid concept of 'need' was replaced by the more fluid concept of 'desire'. Now desire too is being jettisoned in favour of an even more fluid notion, 'wish'. Just as need is constrained by the requirements of the human body, so desire is constrained by social forces that produce conformity, envy and status striving. Wish, however, is unfettered by bodily or social constraints; it is spontaneous and fanciful. No longer forced to adapt to reality, we are free to indulge in the pleasure principle. This ultimate achievement of consumer society is not, Bauman fears, the fulfilment of human potential, but an aimless wallowing in meretricious trivia.

The thesis that a society based on production is giving way to a society based on consumption has faced, I would argue, three main challenges.

First, it is said to rest on a romantic image of an earlier age of work, exaggerating the extent to which workers found deep satisfaction and a strong sense of identity in industrial labour. It generalizes from workers in such industries as mining, steel, the docks and the railways, where work-related community was atypically strong, to industrial settings where workers have always lacked the opportunity to experience collective solidarity.

Second, it underestimates workers' ability to resist managerial attempts to mould the culture of the workplace. Managers devote enormous effort to bringing about cultural change in the workplace. Modern corporations seek to colonize the self. But how far do they succeed?

Third, it draws too sharp a distinction between production and consumption. Instead, following a metaphor proposed by du Gay (1996: 75–95), they should be seen as *imbricated*, that it to say, overlapping like tiles on a roof or scales on a reptile. We cannot understand the world of work unless we examine the orientations that workers bring with them – the values, expectations and priorities that shape their experience of work (Goldthorpe et al. 1969). Equally, we cannot understand the meaning of consumption if we artificially divorce it from the experience of work.

A cultural contradiction between production and consumption?

In *The Cultural Contradictions of Capitalism*, Daniel Bell claims that the ties between the economic system, culture and character have 'unravelled'. Capitalism is being torn apart by contradictions unforeseen by any of the founders of sociology, including Marx.

The crisis of capitalism is caused by conflict between the fundamental (Bell calls them 'axial') principles governing different subsystems within it. Functional rationality is the axial principle of capitalism's technical and economic infrastructure. It involves, as Weber saw, a bureaucratically coordinated quest for rationalized procedures to fit means to ends. To pursue this quest we need a character structure grounded in *this-worldly asceticism*. We must be driven by a 'Protestant' ethic of hard work, thrift and deferred gratification, sacrificing present delights to future fulfilment. We cannot retreat, as hermits and monks do, into other-worldly contemplation. Our work is a calling that we perform as a duty. Even if religious faith declines, this-worldly asceticism is not necessarily undermined, for whereas Puritans believed they had a duty to God, many atheists act out of duty to society. For believers and unbelievers the outcome is the same: a life of self-discipline and self-denial.

The axial principle of contemporary culture, in contrast, is self-expression. Its standards are subjective rather than objective, replacing God's commandments and society's codes of conduct with self-determined tastes and preferences. It celebrates the self as a whole person, and rejects the segmented roles that characterize the division of labour in the techno-economic system. It subordinates instrumentality to expressiveness. It is oriented not to the future but the present.

This explains Bell's preoccupation with the role of hire purchase and consumer credit in contemporary capitalism.

Until well into the twentieth century, banks lent money mainly to businesses rather than to private individuals. Goods were purchased out of income or savings. Buying goods on credit was once a social stigma; now credit cards are widespread, and can even be status symbols – platinum is more illustrious than gold. In the classic slogan, we can 'live now, pay later'. People boast of being 'mortgaged up to the hilt', as if it were heroic. It is the exact opposite of deferred gratification. Instead of sacrificing the present to the future, we mortgage our future to the present. For Bell, this fixation on pleasure-seeking is disastrous. No enduring culture can be founded on self-indulgent immediate gratification.

Like some of the cultural critics discussed below in chapter 3, Bell exaggerates the extent to which American culture has been undermined by 'rampant' consumerism. He laments the passing of the values of small town America, but one might argue that they were largely mythical: small town America was always nostalgically located in the past, never in the present. He accepts without question the notion that consumerism is a field of reckless self-indulgence, in which the use-value of objects is obliterated by their expressive use as status symbols. If, in contrast, we recognize that many consumer activities are practical, utilitarian and goal oriented, the allegedly destructive effect of consumption on the world of work loses credibility.

Even if pleasure-seeking is a powerful strand in consumption, it may not give rise to the contradictions Bell predicts. Hedonism has changed its character, Campbell (1987) argues. In the past, hedonism meant indulging in the pleasures of the senses. Modern hedonism, in contrast, seeks pleasure in the emotions that accompany sensations, and therefore involves imagination, dream and reverie. The consumer is thus a kind of artist.

Hedonism in its modern form is not corrosive of the capitalist mode of production but entirely compatible with it. First, it reconciles workers to the experience of alienated labour. Their daydreaming helps them to cope with the dull compulsions of factory and office work. Second, modern hedonism implies deferred gratification: it is not an ascetic denial of pleasure, but the eager expectation of more intense pleasures in the future. A permanent cycle is set in motion:

desire – acquisition – use – disillusionment – renewed desire. Modern hedonism demands new stimuli, exactly as the economic system requires. Far from being incompatible, production and consumption share the same ethic.

Not only does Bell see culture and structure flying apart, he also argues that consumer culture has become the engine of change. No longer constrained by the imperatives of the techno-economic system, and set free from its moorings in tradition, consumer culture demands new sources of titillation to stimulate its jaded, degenerate appetite. For Bell, consumer culture is internally unstable and functionally incompatible with the technical and economic infrastructure. A more compelling view is that of Bauman, for whom the seductions of consumerism are a mechanism of social control – and devastatingly effective.

The Fordist era: the rise of mass consumption

No product is more richly symbolic of twentieth-century lifestyles than the automobile. It stands for freedom of travel and the exhilaration of driving, but also for alienated labour on the assembly line, traffic congestion, road accidents and environmental pollution. Perhaps it is unsurprising that Henry Ford has been represented as one of the twentieth century's most influential social innovators, the champion of standardized mass production epitomized in the Model T, launched in 1908. His leading role in creating mass consumption has been immortalized in the concept of 'Fordism'.

Fordism was inaugurated in 1914 at Ford's automobile assembly plant in Dearborn, Michigan. Workers were paid the unprecedented sum of 5 dollars for an eight-hour working day. Their work was rationally managed along lines laid down by F. W. ('Speedy') Taylor and other theorists of management 'science'. In return for high pay, workers were expected to surrender discretion at work and submit to the authority of management. Notoriously, Ford established a Sociological Department, whose role was to engineer workers' consent to the rationalized work practices. Ford intended that his 'deal' would undercut the need for unions to represent the interests of organized labour. In the event, unionization of the workforce came to be one of the defining features of the Fordist era. As long as labour organizations focused on 'business unionism', advancing the material interests of their members while leaving management to manage, unions and Fordism could coexist. Union leaders could even fulfil a useful function as 'managers of discontent'.

Fordist mass production of standardized goods required a mass market of consumers to purchase them. This was one reason why Ford paid high wages: he saw that his workers were also his customers. Consumer demand was stimulated by the burgeoning advertising industry, while hire purchase, mortgages and other forms of credit arrangements put goods within the reach of the mass of citizens. Bell sees the expansion of credit as a threat to the spirit of capitalism, but it was a necessary element in the dynamic growth of the capitalist economy. Along with it went mass public provision of welfare services, and economic management by the state to maintain full employment, so that all citizens were capable of discharging their duty as consumers.

The mass market as we know it today began to develop in the United States from the late nineteenth century. It involved a series of closely related trends: the growing impersonality of buyer–seller relations; self-service; advertising; packaging; and the rise of branded goods. This can be told as a story of the evolution of customers into consumers (Strasser 1989: 15).

Impersonality Customers buy commodities from craft workers known personally to them, and from the proprietors of small groceries and general stores. Even as late as 1923, over two-thirds of retail trade in the USA was transacted in Mom-and-Pop stores. Many of the commodities were staple items, unbranded and unpackaged, which the shopkeeper weighed out for the customer. This explains why advertisements for branded goods typically included the caution, 'accept no substitutes'. Such warnings now seem merely quaint, but time was when they addressed the real problem – from the manufacturer's point of view – that shopkeepers were intermediaries between the product and the end user.

Consumers, in contrast, purchase packaged and branded mass-produced goods. These they obtain from impersonal retail outlets. As faith in the shopkeeper was replaced by reliance on the brand, so the power and influence of shopkeepers waned. They gradually lost the capacity to obstruct marketing campaigns by refusing to stock a product or by pushing an alternative brand stacked on shelves behind the counter and out of the customer's reach. As Strasser says, 'No longer were customers to rely on the grocer's opinion about the best soap; no longer could wholesalers choose among various manufacturers who might fulfil their orders. People asked for Ivory, which could only be obtained from Proctor and Gamble' (1989: 30).

Self-service   The first modern self-service store, the Piggly Wiggly, was opened by Clarence Saunders in 1916 in Memphis, Tennessee. The Piggly Wiggly chain eventually grew to 2,660 stores. Self-service enabled retailers to cut costs by ceasing home delivery and shedding labour. It also, crucially, eliminated intermediaries between product and consumer. The pioneering retailing concept of the Piggly Wiggly stores come to fruition in the 1930s, when far larger supermarkets were built on cheap out-of-town land with ample space for parking.

Advertising   In this era, advertising transformed the personal recommendation of the shopkeeper into an endorsement either by a real entrepreneur such as King C. Gillette, inventor of the safety razor, or by fictitious characters such as Uncle Ben and his rice or Aunt Jemima and her Quaker oats. One aim of such campaigns was to establish a quasi-personal tie to the end user, as a surrogate for the proprietor–customer relationship. Equally significant was the effort to obscure the manufacturing process itself, giving a human face to mass production. Aunt Jemima was depicted as a cook who lovingly prepared porridge oats for the family, not a poor African-American woman labouring in a factory.

Packaging   The new relationship between manufacturer and consumer depended on technological developments, not least in packaging. The first machine for manufacturing paper bags was patented in 1852, the first automatic canning factory began operations in 1883, and the manufacture of bottles was fully automated in 1903. Aluminium foil became available from 1910, and cellophane was invented in 1913. Advances in packaging enabled manufacturers to give guarantees about product quality and hygiene. Since customers could no longer see the crackers in the packet, whereas they were used to inspecting the crackers in the barrel, the guarantees took some time to gain acceptance.

Along with these developments went a fusion of product and packaging: the container was no longer a mere vehicle for the product, but integral to it. Packaging became a specialist subject debated in the pages of the American journal *Modern Packaging*, which was launched in 1927 and followed six years later by its British counterpart, *Shelf Appeal* (Bowlby 2000: 80–110). Commodity aesthetics became a contemporary art form, supremely expressed in Raymond Loewy's Coke bottle.

Brands   The rise of branded goods has been a key feature of consumer society. A mere 121 brand names were registered with the US patent office in 1871; by 1906 there were 10,000, and by the early 1920s there were over 50,000 (Norris 1990: 19, cited by Carruthers and Babb 2000: 34). Legislation played a crucial role in supporting the brands. A major advance was made in 1905, when Congress passed a law protecting registered trade marks. Unlike copyright and patents, trade marks have no expiry date. Ten thousand new trade marks were registered within a year of the 1905 Act (Strasser 1989: 45).

The growing significance of trade marks has raised an interesting issue over cases where a brand name becomes the generic word for a whole class of products. For example, 'xerox' is sometimes used as a term for any photocopier, 'hoover' for any vacuum cleaner, and 'coke' for any cola drink. On the face of it, one might expect a corporation to be pleased that their brand has achieved this status, since it reflects their dominant place in the market. Not so: the generic use of trade marks is a liability, not an asset. It shows market leadership but not necessarily brand loyalty. Companies fear what has been called 'genericide': the process by which a trade mark becomes synonymous with all products of its type, as has happened to 'aspirin' and 'escalator'. Genericide means that product differentiation has failed. As Baudrillard argues (1981), branded commodities function as signs whose meaning is produced in a system of relations to other signs. Coca-Cola's claim to be 'the real thing' is meaningful only in relation to Pepsi and other cola drinks. Conversely, 'the Pepsi generation' makes sense only in implicit contrast to a presumably ageing 'Coke generation'. For all their rivalry, Coke and Pepsi need one another.

Genericide blurs the distinction between brands, enabling rival products to trade off the status of the market leader. Retailers are obliged to explain that they do not stock the preferred brand, rather than, say, simply pouring out a Pepsi when a customer asks for a Coke. Advertising slogans often call on consumers to be specific, as in 'Don't say beer, say Bud' and 'Don't be vague, ask for Haig'. At the beginning of the twentieth century, in the early days of Kodak cameras, the company's advertising repeatedly emphasized the message, 'If it isn't an Eastman, it isn't a Kodak'.

A study of thirty-one best selling American novels (Friedman 1985) found that five times as many trade names were used in novels published in the 1970s than in the 1940s. The most commonly cited trade name was Coca-Cola, followed by Cadillac, Ford, Buick, Chevrolet, and Levi. Given the heightened brand consciousness of contemporary consumers, it may be that the problem of genericide is less serious in the twenty-first century than it once was. Even so, trade marks are jealously protected. If they are to keep their trade marks, companies have to show that they take steps to protect them from infringement – hence the threat of litigation hanging over all publications, including this book. Journalists in the UK can verify whether a word is protected by a trade mark by logging on to the Patent Office website at www.patent.gov.uk. *Press Gazette*, the trade paper for British journalists, regularly carries a feature warning that trade marks must be respected, should start with upper-case letters and be spelled 'correctly' – not portacabin, but Portakabin. The House of Chanel goes further, demanding that its products be upper-case throughout, as in 'a CHANEL suit'. Not every worm drive hose clip, an advertisement reminds the reader, is entitled to be called a Jubilee clip.

Many of America's and the world's most famous brands date from the late nineteenth and early twentieth century. Examples are Quaker oats, Shredded Wheat, Uncle Ben's rice, Campbell's soup, Heinz 57 varieties, Wrigley's chewing gum, Jell-O jelly, Waterman pens, Kodak cameras, Colgate toothpaste, Carnation milk, Kellogg's cornflakes, and Coca-Cola.

This list of successful brands is a catalogue of everyday items that are embedded in the lifestyles of First World societies. Many signify national identity, which is why émigrés and exiles typically yearn for them. What could be more American than an Oreo cookie, more French than Suze, more British than Jacob's Cream Crackers or more Australian than Vegemite? Their symbolic value is shown by the evidence of foreigners, who are usually unimpressed if they try these national delicacies.

The structures of mass production and mass consumption are deceptively precarious. For all its apparent strengths, the Fordist era – according to writers in the French 'regulationist' school who forged the concept of Fordism (for example, Aglietta 1979; Lipietz 1987) – has been undermined by its own inherent contradictions. Capitalism requires production and consumption to be aligned with each other, but alignment does not come about automatically. Contrary to the theories of neoclassical economics, there is no long-run tendency towards equilibrium. Instead, capitalism is subject to recurrent crises out of which new alignments of consumption and production are born.

The collapse of Fordism

The heyday of Fordism, most writers agree, was the sustained economic boom from the end of the Second World War in 1945 to the oil crisis and recession of 1973. Since then, we have allegedly entered the era of post-Fordist flexible specialization.

Ford's iconic Model T was reliable and cheap, but also unashamedly functional and ugly. Aesthetics did not count.

Only luxury vehicles produced by craft systems of production could enjoy the frills of designer aesthetics. Henry Ford famously said of the 1914 Model T: 'Any customer can have a car painted any color he wants as long as it is black.'

Ford's well-known statement points to the irony of singling him out as the genius of consumer capitalism. In the 1920s, the success story of automobile manufacture was not Ford but General Motors (Gartman 1994). GM offered its customers cars with *style*. Models were redesigned annually, encouraging consumers to change their car frequently to keep up with the latest fashions. Annual redesign was an important element in the strategy of planned obsolescence, which ensured that consumer demand remained buoyant. It implied that the owners of an automobile are not simply rational actors who have purchased a means of transport, but communicators (or dupes) who want to convey symbolic messages about their social status – messages that need regular updating as the field of symbols is continually manipulated by the manufacturers (Bauman 2000: 85). Fittingly for a socially mobile society, the different marques that made up the GM model range were constructed in a stylistic hierarchy: Chevrolet for the blue-collar masses, Oldsmobile for the middle classes, Buick for the affluent and Cadillac for the rich. Moving up the GM range was a way of fulfilling the American dream.

There may well be mythical elements in the notion that the first half of the twentieth century was the era of 'Fordism'. Mythical or not, surely the First World has now moved beyond the mass production of standardized products and entered an age of 'flexible specialization'? Information technology makes it possible to combine high output with far shorter runs of particular products, and to customize them to suit the requirements of individual consumers. In 1914, the Model T was available in black only, whereas today's Ford Focus is produced not simply in a wide palette but also with different engines, various levels of trim and all manner of optional accessories. In the global marketplace the consumer is sovereign, and no major company can succeed unless it is able to meet individual requirements and respond quickly to changes in consumer demand.

According to many commentators, the transition from Fordism to flexible specialization has brought about the collapse of social class, political party, local community and the world of work as sources of identity. In the case of the United Kingdom, for example, political scientists have identified a process of *partisan dealignment*. Fewer British citizens feel a strong sense of identification with a political party; many are willing to decide afresh at each election which party to vote for – if any. Political socialization through the family has declined, so that when people vote differently from their parents they are unlikely to be labelled as traitors to their social origins. The communal basis of political parties at local level has been eroded. The local party is not so much a source of sociability and a vehicle of political participation as a machine periodically mobilized to win elections. This shift from *Gemeinschaft* (community) to *Gesellschaft* (association) in grassroots politics is tellingly illustrated in France and other European countries by the fall of communism. The CGT (Confédération Générale du Travail), the communist-aligned trade union, lost over two-thirds of its membership in the 1970s and 1980s. In the eyes of its disillusioned activists, the CGT has substituted administration for politics (Bourdieu et al. 1999: 317–20). With the end of the Cold War and the collapse of communism, the old left–right allegiances arguably have less meaning.

Partisan dealignment is paralleled by *class dealignment*. The link between social class and political allegiance has weakened, partly because of the decline of the industrial working class and the heavy industries that gave rise to strong communities of solidarity in adversity.

Partisan and class dealignment are part of a wider process of detraditionalization, signalling a change in the way culture is transmitted from generation to generation. The provision of expert professional advice illustrates this, nowhere more graphically than in the field of personal financial services (Burton 1994). Customers are encouraged to relate to their bank impersonally via cash machines, the telephone and the internet. Once a trusted personal adviser to a family, the bank manager has disappeared from view. Few people identify with 'their' bank. Although they may be reluctant to switch banks, this is not loyalty but inertia.

Similar developments have occurred in the unlikely field of religion, which has been influenced by the values and practices of consumer society. Even the Roman Catholic Church has been profoundly affected. The authority of the priesthood has declined, so that lay people increasingly choose which aspects of Catholic teaching to follow and which to ignore – notably the warnings against artificial means of contraception. As for religious socialization, Hervieu-Léger's work in France shows that fewer Catholics feel obliged to transmit their faith to their children as a cultural birthright (Hervieu-Léger 2000). Adopting a more pluralist view of religious affiliation, they believe that religious socialization involves bringing children up in such a way that they can make well-informed choices for themselves.

Detraditionalization implies that the current generation has loosened its ties to its predecessors, as one would expect consumers to do. If consumers feel less indebted to earlier generations, can they expect their descendants to behave any differently? Consumer society cannot rupture its ties to the past while leaving intact its links to the future.

Perhaps the most vivid illustration of this is the problem of income in retirement. Put bluntly, the Fordist worker was expected to retire at sixty-five and die shortly thereafter. His widow would then eke out their savings for a few more years. Given this scenario, and given a full employment economy, pensions could be financed on a pay-as-you-go basis, that is to say, paid for not by the lifetime contributions of people in retirement but out of current taxation. The post-Fordist worker, in contrast, enjoys increased life expectancy, and this is producing a greying population of retired people financially dependent on those still in work. In some countries, for example Japan, Germany, France and Italy, the dependent population is predicted to outnumber the working population by the middle of this century (N. Ferguson 2001: 219). This is why so many countries have identified pension reform as a priority. The objective is to fund workers' retirement income mainly from their own contributions built up over their working life, rather than from taxes raised by the state. It is not the state but the state pension that is withering away. In the United Kingdom, a significant move by the neoliberal Thatcher administration in the 1980s was to sever the link between the state pension and average earnings, substituting a less valuable link with the index of retail prices. A massive financial burden, and the associated financial risk, is being transferred not simply from the state to the individual, but from future generations to the present. Income in retirement is a major source of insecurity in the post-Fordist world. It is not unconnected to insecurity at work, to which we now turn.

The end of career

If our working life is to be characterized as 'a career', it implies a cumulative achievement, an orderly ascent up a ladder of opportunity. Career requires stable employment and predictable upward mobility. Careers are most fully developed in bureaucracies and professions, both of which protect their members against the full force of the free market. Manual and routine clerical workers who lack opportunities for career advancement can still enjoy the benefits of job security – a horizontal career of stable employment provided by large organizations, protected by labour unions, and cushioned by the full employment policies of the welfare state.

People who have careers typically show commitment and loyalty, whether to a particular employer, an industry, a craft or a profession. They take pride in their work, deriving a sense of identity from it. They are conscious of themselves as members of an occupational community, either locally based, as in the case of heavy industry, or more cosmopolitan, as with the professions and the crafts.

All this has vanished along with the Fordist bargain and the Fordist state. Careers are no longer guaranteed but *contingent* – 'where current performance is the only valid criterion for reward and punishment' (M. Aldridge 2001). Pay is determined by performativity, not seniority or collective agreements. Organizations are delayered, removing rungs from the ladder of opportunity. Contracts of employment are individualized. The modern corporation insists that employees must be flexible, and no longer even pretends to offer job security.

In attempting to break free from dependency on labour, capital puts itself at the service of global consumerism (Bauman 2000: 130–67). Globalization means the end of career (Kanter 1993). It also demands that social institutions perpetually reinvent themselves. Although inherently chaotic and seemingly pointless, corporate re-engineering is a rational response to globalization. As Sennett says, 'Perfectly viable businesses are gutted or abandoned, capable employees are set adrift rather than rewarded, simply because the organization must prove to the market that it is capable of change' (1998: 51). Disruption is surprisingly profitable, bringing substantial benefits to corporate executives and shareholders, at least in the short term.

Reflecting the growing contingency of careers, the concept of job security has been replaced by the idea that security lies in being *employable*. Employability is not achieved by building up a stock of traditional skills, since capitalism continually negates the skills of the past. Older workers cannot pass on accumulated skills to the next generation. Even apparently leading-edge skills rapidly become obsolete, and yesterday's jobs for life are today's dim memories – for example the TV repair man.

How can employees solve the problem of predicting which skills will be needed in future? Two strategies suggest themselves. First, avoid skills linked to specific technologies and concentrate on the skills of interpersonal communication. These skills will be 'transferable' from one employment setting to the next. They are the core skills needed by consultants, trainers and facilitators. Second, cultivate your contacts, 'networking' with people who may one day give you a job. As Pahl observes, 'Jobs that plug into valuable networks are better than jobs that are tied to potentially outdated skills and work-related experiences' (1995: 3).

According to Sennett (1998), the death of Fordism has had dire consequences for our working lives. We have fewer long-term relationships, giving us no outlet for loyalty, commitment and trust. Our greater flexibility does not enrich our sensibilities, but renders us amoral. Hence the title of

Sennett's book: *The Corrosion of Character*. In a consumer society our orientation to work is instrumental and calculative (Goldthorpe et al. 1969). Work is a means to an end, a field not of moral engagement but rational calculation of personal advantage. We may work in so-called 'teams', but these are relationships 'of demeaning superficiality' (Sennett 1998: 99). Workers are obliged to make a show of identifying with the team, but they do not internalize its demands. Survival means putting on a mask of cooperativeness.

Even if this analysis is accepted it does not rule out hope. Sennett himself (1998: 148) argues that no social order can survive unless it provides people with reasons to care about one another. The post-Fordist era of flexible specialization bears the seeds of its own destruction, since few people are really committed to it. It is a sham, and people will not support it when it crumbles.

Why, in any case, should we look back nostalgically to a golden age of Fordism? It may have produced admirable solidarity among workers, but this was to resist Fordism, not endorse it. As Gorz points out (1999: 4), neoliberalism triumphed precisely because the working class rejected the hegemony of Fordism and the bureaucratic welfare state. Many aspects of the neoliberal agenda were popular with labour as well as capital. The collapse of Fordism opens up the possibility of a liberation that cannot be achieved within capitalism. Capitalist post-Fordism demands that workers internalize the corporate culture unquestioningly – a latter-day variant of feudalism. It offers only a virtual emancipation, not a real one.

Job insecurity may, therefore, mark the demise of the 'work-based society'. ' "Work" must lose its centrality in the minds, thoughts and imaginations of everyone' (Gorz 1999: vii). It always was a social construct, not an anthropological universal: hence its abolition is possible. There is mounting evidence of the dislocation of 'work' and 'life'. Politicians have been slow to recognize the growing discontent; they mistake people's attachment to the rights and entitlements derived from employment for a personal investment in employment itself. Politicians have ironically become more inclined to promote employment, as in the welfare-to-work programmes in the USA and the UK. What people long for, in contrast, is 'a more relaxed, more multi-active life' (Gorz 1999: 64). We need a political blueprint for a society of 'chosen time' and 'multi-activity'. In such a society, the conflict between work and leisure, production and consumption, will be resolved by the abolition of the false dichotomy.

Gorz's critics judge this to be utopian.

The corporate embrace: narcissism and emotional labour

Many writers have commented on the tendency of modern corporations to undermine autonomous workplace culture. Established ways of working are dismissed as inefficient restrictive practices. Mechanisms by which workplace culture was passed from generation to generation, as in the traditional apprenticeship system, are demolished (Strangleman and Roberts 1999). The aim is to create a cultural 'ground zero', after which workers can be socialized into an irresistible managerial culture. In the new order, as du Gay (1996) comments, the goals of enterprising employees and the goals of the corporation are one.

Such, at least, is the vision of management gurus who follow Peters and Waterman (1982) in search of corporate excellence. Some critics despair at the corporate colonization of the self, while others argue that it is a brittle sham that cannot last for long.

Lasch's analysis of the culture of narcissism (see pp. 75–8 below) profoundly influenced Casey's (1995) study of the pseudonymous Hephaestus Corporation, which manufactures IT systems. Casey paints a portrait of corporate psychopathology. Hephaestus's corporate 'identity' as a harmonious team or happy family conceals an oppressive reality of colonization of the self. It preaches self-development, but subjects its employees to a regime of surveillance and intimidation.

Narcissism is rooted in the failure to distinguish one's self from one's environment. By seeking to obliterate the distinction between self and corporation, the corporate project of colonization of the self is therefore an agent of narcissism.

Faced with this project what is the employee to do? Casey
analyses three options:

- *Defence*
Defence involves collective solidarity in opposition to the
corporation's project of colonization. According to Casey,
capitalism has reconstituted itself in such a way that collective defence has been fatally wounded. The passing of
the Fordist era has seen a collapse of collective solidarity.
- *Collusion*
Collusion, whether compulsive or passive, is what the corporation seeks. Compliant, dependent and ambitious, the
colluded employee has bought into corporate ideology.
Collusion entails a brittle 'onward and upward' form of
optimism.
- *Capitulation*
This is the main strategy for defending the self. It takes
two forms. In its pragmatic mode, the employee adopts
an air of ironic detachment and cynicism as a means of
self-protection. Pragmatists are sustained by the belief
that if their job became intolerable they could find work
elsewhere. The reluctant mode is where weary former
defensives and disenchanted colluders finish up, with
more doubts than the pragmatists.

These three options draw on Hirschman's influential
analysis of ways of responding to unsatisfactory situations
(Hirschman 1970). First, people may seek a *voice*. In a corporation, workers might find a voice through consultative
committees, union representation, complaints procedures or
legal redress. Second, workers may choose *loyalty*, revising
their expectations and adjusting to the situation. Finally,
workers may opt for *exit*, by changing their job within the
corporation or leaving it altogether.

Casey's analysis is pessimistic, allowing little scope for
worker resistance. Defence/voice has been undermined by
the logic of mass consumerism, and in many companies has
ceased to be a serious option. It exists only as romantic nostalgia for a lost world of union power.

Collusion/loyalty is risky. Loyalty is what the corporation
asks for, but will the worker be rewarded for it? The corpo-

ration appeals to a revamped work ethic, but the condition of contemporary capitalism means that it cannot guarantee to deliver an orderly career and a job for life. The loyal, colluded employee risks the shock of betrayal – a fate that has befallen many employees in Japan, some of whom go to extraordinary trouble to conceal from their families the disgrace of having been fired.

Capitulation/exit is precarious. It might be argued that exit is always on offer in the market economy, and that the market's legitimacy depends on it. It is the familiar justification: if you don't like it, go elsewhere. Casey points out, however, that as workers advance through middle age their prospects for exit diminish. The possibility of escape from the corporate embrace becomes an ever more desperate myth. Unable to achieve exit, workers opt for internal exile. Denied the exercise of free choice, they adopt the psychological defence mechanism of denial – denial that they have become victims.

Narcissistic corporations breed self-congratulation and illusions of invulnerability. Not satisfied with mere compliance, the corporation demands an evangelistic celebration of corporate culture. Obsessed by image, corporate executives mistake rhetoric for the reality from which it is in fact a flight. Many employees – Casey's capitulators – respond cynically. Gabriel (1999: 209) points out that cynicism is helpful for narcissistic corporations. Cynics are held up to employees as folk devils – wreckers, dinosaurs, the enemy within.

What, though, has caused modern corporations to attempt to colonize their employees' self? Why is it not enough that workers turn up on time and meet their production targets without giving any trouble to the people in charge of them? That is all that Scientific Management required. If capitalism is governed by the cash nexus, why the effort to manipulate employees' emotions under the pretence of caring for them?

The answer may be found in the logic of consumer society and the centrality of the service sector. The ideology of consumer sovereignty has invaded the world of work, so that more and more people have their jobs defined as meeting the needs of the customer. In pursuit of customer satisfaction, workers are encouraged to regard work as something that they themselves consume. Dealings between individuals and departments within the corporation are restructured as consumer–producer, purchaser–provider relations. Work is imagined as an arena in which workers pursue personal lifestyle projects, and managers claim that their role is to empower workers to do this (du Gay 1996: 76–80). An instrumental and calculative orientation to work, as found among factory workers in the classic *Affluent Worker* studies of the 1960s (Goldthorpe et al. 1969), is not permissible in a corporation dedicated to serving the demands of the sovereign consumer.

The man on the assembly line, as Arlie Hochschild remarks, is an outdated symbol of alienated labour. For a contemporary symbol, we should consider women and men delivering services in face-to face or voice-to-voice encounters with the public. Service workers must engage in what Hochschild calls *emotional labour*, which she defines as 'the management of feeling to create publicly observable facial and bodily display', adding that 'emotional labour is sold for a wage and therefore has *exchange value*' (Hochschild 1983: 7n). This emotional labour is part of the service itself.

Emotional labour involves acting out a part – and here a crucial distinction needs to be made. In *surface acting*, workers try to change their outward appearance through their use of body language. Surface acting is relatively unproblematic for those obliged to engage in it: it is a superficial performance, and recognized as such. In a consumer society we are adept at detecting these displays and discounting them. We know service workers are obliged to wish us a nice day, and in a civilized manner we normally reciprocate politely.

In *deep acting*, workers strive to alter their feelings, so that they really experience genuine and deep concern for their clients. Workers are schooled to treat their place of work as their home, and to relate to clients as though they were family members or close friends for whom they felt genuine affection.

Deep acting may be corrosive of interpersonal relations and dangerous to the actor. Hochschild considers three possibilities (1983: 187). First, as with Casey's colluders, workers may over-identify with the job, running the risk of stress and

burnout. They may easily feel rejected, and can be hyper-
sensitive to criticism – characteristics displayed, for example,
by front-line social workers (M. Aldridge 1994: 182). Second,
workers may try to maintain a clear distinction between self
and job, at the risk of feeling guilty about being hypocritical.
Third, workers may distinguish self from job without
blaming themselves or feeling guilty about it. The outcome
may be cynicism.

Hochschild's main case study was of flight attendants
working for Delta Airlines, a non-union company with a high
reputation for service to the customer. Delta's formal train-
ing included intensive instruction in emotional labour. In
other institutional settings, for example hospitals and hos-
pices, the skills of emotional labour are not formally taught
but have to be picked up on the job (James 1989). In the
caring professions, emotional labour may well be regarded
as coming 'naturally' to women and not being 'real' work at
all. Delta Airlines, a commercial operator, recognized
women's emotional labour and paid for it. A question for
cultural critics is to determine where the greater exploitation
lies.

Most commentators have overlooked Hochschild's case
study of debt collectors (Hochschild 1983: 137–47), but it is
no less significant. This is the dark side of consumer society,
and overwhelmingly a man's world (though the few women
debt collectors enjoy the advantage of taking customers by
surprise). Their task is not to make customers feel better, but
to denigrate them. Far from being a problem, customer complaints are interpreted as a sign that the debt collector is doing
his job properly. Debt collectors use anger, distrust and intimidation to induce their 'clients' to feel so guilty or afraid that
they clear their debt. As with flight attendants, the employer
wants deep rather than surface acting. Debt collectors are
trained to despise their clients, who are not the deserving
poor struggling to make ends meet but idlers, cheats and
'welfare bums'. Even more so than flight attendants, debt
collectors run the risk that their human sensibilities will be
coarsened beyond repair.

The discourse of service and
the quest for authenticity

Consumer society has brought fundamental shifts in public discourse. One of the most striking elements of this is the rise of *conversationalization* (Fairclough 1994), in which public discourse is modelled on the language of private life.

Both in their internal workings and in their communication with customers, corporations insist relentlessly on informal styles that were once reserved for intimate relationships. A symbol of this is the proliferation of first names. Total strangers phone you at home, announce that they are Judy or Justin, and may even call you Alan. To demand a more formal mode of address would be hopelessly pompous, while asking them out for a drink would be to misinterpret the rules of the game and might constitute harassment.

Does conversationalization matter? Heavy corporate investment in discourse as part of the programme of culture management suggests that we cannot dismiss it out of hand. Corporate executives may be irrational dupes, but shareholders expect them to be rational actors and demand a return on their investment. We should at least entertain the possibility that conversationalization serves a purpose.

If it does, is it good or bad? Here Fairclough points to a dilemma. On the one hand, conversationalization is a calculated ploy used instrumentally to exploit its target. Justin is selling double-glazing, and Judy is a financial adviser who wants to take a percentage for managing my money. I cannot really blame them for their simulated conversational style since they are following a script, as we all know. On the other hand, as a customer I want friendly service, and informality suggests that we share a common bond as human beings and as equal citizens of a democracy. Conversationalization may be read as a product of the decline of deference and status distinction.

Conversationalization is simultaneously engineered and democratic. It is 'a focus of struggles to substantively democratize society and on the other hand to maintain existing hegemonic relations through a semblance of democratization' (Fairclough 1994: 266) – illustrating a profound cultural ambivalence over the authority of the consumer. Consumers' responses to it oscillate between trust and cynicism. One strategy for coping with the ambivalence is endemic – irony.

In her study of telephone call centres, Cameron analyses two aspects of corporate discourse. *Verbal hygiene* refers to efforts to cleanse the language of inappropriate elements, so that it conforms to a given standard of correctness, clarity, efficiency, beauty or morality. *Styling* refers to the grooming of appearance, managing the aesthetics of interaction, for example by cultivating a 'warm' voice (Cameron 2000: 86–9). Not only does styling fail to equip people with genuine skills and expertise, it does not even give much insight into the principles of social interaction. It is an exercise in compliance, teaching employees to discipline their verbal and non-verbal behaviour so that they can function more efficiently within the organization in pursuit of its goals.

Verbal hygiene and styling are imposed on subordinates by people further up the hierarchy. Staff appraisals are devised in order to compel employees to use the new linguistic register. As Cameron drily remarks (2000: 15–16), 'Since appraisal is typically compulsory, and often consequential in terms of pay and promotion, everyone has an interest in mastering the quasi-therapeutic register associated with it.'

Hochschild found that service workers are often disturbed by the emotional labour required of them. Cameron's study confirms this. Her work on call centres demonstrates the pressures of enacting a synthetic personality and reciting a banal script. One problem is that customers are not obliged to reciprocate, and many are rude. Attending to the emotional needs of the customer can be at the expense of one's own.

Even more troubling is the question of authenticity. Surface acting may not matter, but deep acting does. Both as producers and as consumers, we have an interest in distinguishing the genuine from the fake. This may mean that the disjunction between production and consumption is less stable than sometimes thought.

3

Consumer Society: Utopia or Dystopia?

Explicitly or implicitly, social science offers us descriptions, visions and blueprints of the good society. Even when it claims to be realistic its utopian strand is unmissable. Although it may be unscientific, utopianism addresses fundamental aspects of human society: crime and punishment, eugenics, euthanasia, sex and gender, animal rights, justice – and, not least, production and consumption. Without a utopian vision of a better world we may find no antidote to despair.

The term 'utopia', literally meaning 'nowhere', was coined by Sir Thomas More in his tract *Utopia*, published in 1516. Over time its meaning has shifted (Carey 1999: xi). It is now commonly used to mean a *good* place, possibly because of confusion with the Greek prefix eu-, meaning 'well' or 'good', as in euphoria, an overwhelming sense of well-being, and eugenics, the science of improving the 'race'. Because of this change of meaning, the word 'dystopia' was invented to connote a bad place. Utopia expresses desire, dystopia fear.

In twentieth-century writing the dystopian strand predominated, as in Aldous Huxley's *Brave New World* (published 1932) and George Orwell's *1984* (published 1949). Apparent utopias typically conceal a grotesque secret. A classic case is Harry Harrison's science fiction novel *Make Room! Make Room!*, later filmed as *Soylent Green*. An overpopulated society has developed a nutritious food, soylent green, which unknown to consumers is manufactured from human corpses. It is the ultimate consumer horror: cannibalism.

'Utopian' is also used to refer to hopes that are groundless. When Marx and Engels wrote disparagingly of utopian socialism in *The Communist Manifesto* of 1848, they meant that it was simply wishful thinking. Their own socialism, they believed, was grounded in the science of society, a science which demonstrates the inevitable progress of history to socialism and ultimately, as the state withers away, to full communism.

Marx and Engels have, of course, themselves been accused of utopianism by self-styled 'realists'. Given that this is an often repeated pattern of debate, it suggests that the distinction between realism and utopianism is, as Arblaster and Lukes argue, 'a misleading and value-loaded, indeed polemical distinction, serving to conceal the value premises from which it is made' (1971: 10).

Futuristic utopian thought normally envisages a radical reordering of production and consumption. In Edward Bellamy's *Looking Backward, 2000–1887* (1951/1888), private property and money have been abolished – a typical utopian move. Everyone is issued with a credit card representing an equal share of the annual national product; this must be spent within the year, since savings cannot be accumulated. From age twenty-one to forty-five, people are enlisted in 'the industrial army' and engage in productive labour under tight military discipline. They then retire, to enjoy the happiest years of their life – as consumers!

Accepting Bellamy's egalitarianism but rejecting his love of regimentation, William Morris depicts in *News from Nowhere* (1970/1890) a society in which goods are not sold but given away. Power is decentralized and cities are returned to nature, processes memorably symbolized by the transformation of London's Houses of Parliament into a fruit and vegetable market.

Oscar Wilde remarked that 'A map of the world that does not include utopia is not even worth glancing at . . .' (1891). The question remains, would we choose to live there?

A utopia for consumers: free market capitalism

The twentieth century saw the ascendancy of 'the market' in Western discourse about society. Following Carrier (1997: 47–54), we can think of market discourse as a modern *lingua franca*, a public language adopted as a means of communication between different groups and strata in society. English is now the international *lingua franca* of science, technology and business, just as French was once the *lingua franca* of diplomacy and Latin the *lingua franca* of Christendom. In our own times, the language of 'the market' threatens to become the dominant *lingua franca* through which the social order is discussed and understood.

Far from being a neutral medium of communication, the language of the market is ideologically charged, not only motivating action and legitimizing institutions but defining reality. Social relations do not become *like* market relations between buyers and sellers, they *are* market relations. A simile is transformed into a metaphor (López 2003).

This metaphor, critics say, has run riot. It may not be surprising that people who work in the City of London simply take it as axiomatic that markets are the most efficient and equitable way of allocating resources. For them, state regulation and investor protection are unwarranted interference with the free and beneficial play of market forces (Lazar 1990). More telling is that other sectors of society, such as schools and universities, in which the metaphor of the market used to be anathema, have now embraced it. Even religious organizations have succumbed (A. Aldridge 2000). The metaphor shapes more than our talk; it colonizes our thinking and practice.

The market is a compound of three elements: a *description* of how things are, an abstract *analytic model* generated within economic theory, and a *prescription* for how human affairs ought to be conducted. It has the following key features.

Individualism   The individual is an autonomous agent whose wants, expressed as consumer demand, are what powers the economy. One paradoxical way of expressing this is to say that the consumer is 'a hero of modernity' (Slater 1997: 33–62). It is not the lofty ideals of intellectuals but the everyday desires of common humanity that drive modernity forward. Knowledgeable consumers pursuing their self-interest find their counterparts in risk-taking entrepreneurs eager to satisfy consumer demand. Instead of being exceptional, consumers and entrepreneurs are everyday heroes.

Instrumental rationality   Modern heroes are motivated by the rational pursuit of enlightened self-interest. Consumers are not dependent on guidance from social superiors, nor are they slaves to dark irrational passions. Self-aware, self-disciplined and mature, they are autonomous agents seeking the most effective means of achieving goals they have freely chosen. This is the form of rationality that Max Weber termed *Zweckrationalität*, instrumental rationality, and it was rationality of this type that he saw as dominant in the modern world.

Efficiency   In a free market economy, resource allocation is determined entirely by the interplay of supply and demand as expressed through prices. The price mechanism sends signals about the relative value consumers place on goods and services (demand) and the relative costs of producing and delivering them (supply). Prices provide incentives to increase profitable activities and decrease unprofitable ones. Because it reflects the innumerable decisions of countless actors in the marketplace, the price mechanism is a far more accurate reflection of social realities than any centrally planned economy could possibly achieve. The amount of information that would be needed by central planners is far too great for them to gather and process it effectively.

Freedom   The market breeds autonomous, enterprising, self-reliant people. An extreme form is found in the ideology of survivalists and anti-government militias in the USA. In the mainstream, we find the American dream's populist image of 'the little guy' who stands a chance of getting on in life provided government bureaucracy gets off his back. Freedom from interference – 'negative liberty', Isaiah Berlin called it (1969) – is a core principle of liberalism.

Choice As well as 'negatively' free from constraint, people are 'positively' free to choose from an array of goods and services. Choice is essential to the functioning of the market, and is experienced as desirable: the more the better objectively and subjectively. As Lebergott bluntly says: 'In open societies, human consumption choices share only one characteristic – they are made in pursuit of happiness' (1993: 11). He goes on to claim that economists are right to assume that human wants are insatiable.

Prosperity Growing prosperity is an outcome of the efficiency of the market. Market societies are affluent societies, with the United States in the lead. Twentieth-century American consumers, according to Lebergott (1993: xi), were 'spending their way towards happiness'. Affordable automobiles were the key to the highway, while the diffusion of labour-saving devices liberated women from heavy domestic toil. Centrally planned economies, in contrast, are irredeemably inefficient and corrupt. They do not encourage their citizens to travel, and they glorify drudgery.

Dynamism The market unleashes a torrent of technological and organizational innovation that destroys old social and cultural forms – what the economist Joseph Schumpeter (1961) called 'creative destruction'. The free market punishes sloth and complacency, rewarding people who are enterprising, energetic and adaptable. New technologies and new products continually make old skills redundant.

Consumption The market society is by its very nature a consumer society. Consumer satisfaction is maximized when entrepreneurs compete for custom in a free market. Contrast this with the image of the bureaucratic state sector, or worse, with the command economy, whose sullen functionaries are licensed to be rude to the queues of weary people they are supposed to be serving.

The ascendancy of the market as practice and discourse has many causes. First, the neoliberal governments of the 1980s, particularly in the USA under Ronald Reagan and the UK under Margaret Thatcher, were determined to promote free markets and to eradicate all obstacles to them, including the monopolistic practices of trade unions and professional associations.

Second, deindustrialization and the growth of the service economy have contributed to the dominance of market imagery. Public attention has switched from manufacturing, now stigmatized as the smokestack industries and metal-bashing of 'the old economy', to the service sector and the progressive 'new economy' centred on technology, media and telecommunications. The stock market represents itself as the symbolic dynamo of this new economy.

Third, Fordism has collapsed, bringing an end to the so-called 'Fordist bargain', in which workers were compensated for the rigours of mass production by high wages and job security. The Fordist era has passed; mass production has given way to flexible specialization, with products customized to the tastes of individual consumers. The guarantee of job security is acknowledged to be unrealistic in an age of fierce and incessant global competition.

Fourth, social class is said to be a casualty of deindustrialization and the passing of Fordism. Close-knit occupational communities have declined along with the industries, such as coal, steel and the docks, which created and sustained them. People's sense of their own identity and that of others is shaped less by their work than by the goods and services they consume.

Fifth, the end of communism in the Soviet Union and East-Central Europe is represented as the victory of the free market over the planned economy. The newly liberated people clamoured not only for liberty, but for Western goods and lifestyles. Communism, like Western socialism, is pronounced a utopian vision that has decisively failed.

Sixth, the social processes outlined above have brought with them a disorientation and even a collapse of confidence among Western Marxists. Discourse about 'capitalism' risks seeming hopelessly out of touch with contemporary realities. Principled resistance to the idealization of Western market economies has been undermined – or at least temporarily dislocated.

Hence we arrive, finally, at what Fukuyama (1992) calls 'the end of history'. Having defeated the challenge of fascism and communism, free market capitalism faces no serious opposition.

Yet surely markets do not always deliver the literal and metaphorical goods? Even neoclassical economists recognize the problem of 'market failure', where market performance falls short of the ideal. It is a situation in which market prices fail to reflect social costs and benefits. Since supply is not matched to demand, resources are not allocated efficiently. The following are among problems that cause markets to fail.

Monopoly Where one supplier captures a market (monopoly), or where a few suppliers succeed in restricting competition (oligopoly), goods and services will be undersupplied and overpriced.

Lack of information If consumers do not have sufficient information on which to base their choice of goods and services, inferior goods and services will drive out superior ones. In Akerlof's (1970) famous example, the market for second-hand cars will be dominated by unreliable vehicles unless consumers can tell a good car from a 'lemon'.

Externalities The perfect market requires that producers bear all the costs of production and their customers gain all the benefits of consumption. An external diseconomy occurs when producers are able to escape bearing costs, such as car manufactures avoiding the cost of traffic congestion or chemical plants the cost of pollution. External costs are not reflected in prices, so goods are underpriced and oversupplied. Conversely, external economies mean that producers are not getting the full benefit of their enterprise; hence goods will be overpriced and undersupplied.

Public goods In the economist's terms, public goods have two problematic qualities. They are non-excludable, that is, nobody can be prevented from benefiting from them: for example, clean air and national defence. They are also non-rivalrous, in that one person's enjoying them does not prevent others from doing so. These characteristics mean that they cannot be supplied by private firms for sale on the market. Instead they are typically financed either by altruistic voluntary activity or by government taxation. If it were left to the market, public goods would be undersupplied or not supplied at all.

Although advocates of the free market recognize the phenomenon of market failure, they seek in various ways to limit its importance. For one thing, some market failure is relatively mild, and if state intervention is the cure it may prove far worse than the problem. However well intentioned, and however politically persuasive, state regulation typically produces severe market distortions and a seriously inefficient allocation of resources.

Advocates of the market argue that not only is state intervention counterproductive, it usually lacks even a semblance of justification, because market failure is often mythical. Two cases will illustrate this. First, there is a widespread opinion that the VHS video format won the battle with Beta despite the fact the Beta was the superior technology. VHS, the story goes, dominated the market early on through efficient marketing. Consumers chose VHS not because it was superior but simply because it was the market leader. People wanted to be able to exchange tapes with their friends, and they wanted a wide choice of films to hire from the video shops. Consumers were locked in to the inferior VHS format because of these market distortions.

According to two American economists, Liebowitz and Margolis (1990), this story does not stand up to scrutiny. Beta was not superior to VHS; they were technically very similar. Beta was launched before VHS, which ought to have given it a crucial advantage. However, in developing the Beta format the Sony Corporation made a fatal error. Mistakenly thinking that consumers wanted cassettes to be small and easily portable, they sacrificed playing time to size. Sony's rival, Matsushita, chose a larger tape format that offered a longer playing time. The myth is market failure, the truth is the market delivering to consumers what they wanted.

The second case is the so-called 'universal' or Sholes type-writer keyboard, patented in 1868 and known in English-speaking countries as QWERTY and in some others as AZERTY. The QWERTY layout, so we have been told, was deliberately designed by its inventor, Christopher Sholes, to prevent secretaries from typing so quickly that the hammers jammed. The keyboard layout was inefficient by design, yet well over a century later it remains the standard. A more efficient keyboard has been designed, the Dvorak layout, but even though it is far superior it has not caught on. QWERTY dominates the market because it established an early lead that became unassailable once thousands and then millions of typists were trained to use QWERTY and only QWERTY.

There is, however, no hard evidence, according to Liebowitz and Margolis (1995), that the Dvorak layout is a significant improvement on QWERTY. Some methodologically flawed experiments were carried out in the 1930s, which claimed to show a pay-back within ten days from a switch to Dvorak. These experiments were designed and overseen for the US navy by its time and motion expert, Lieutenant Commander August Dvorak. His findings have never been replicated.

Any true believer in the market would have been sceptical about these two myths, since they depend on the assumption that competition does not operate because entrepreneurs and consumers are idle and stupid. If VHS were so inferior to Beta, surely consumers would have found it out very quickly and stopped buying the inferior product? And if switching to the Dvorak keyboard would pay for itself in ten days, how can it be that profit-maximizing capitalist firms have not rushed to cut their costs?

Why, then, are the myths so entrenched? The answer, according to Liebowitz and Margolis, is that they appeal to the prejudices of left-wing intellectuals, who cannot believe that mere entrepreneurs and a mass market of consumers could possibly produce the good society. Utopia has to be planned, and who better to do the planning than intellectuals?

Liebowitz and Margolis may themselves not escape the charge of ideological blinkers. They and others like them are remarkably resistant to any suggestion that markets are less than perfect. Their advocacy shades over into what Frank (2001) has called 'market populism', by which he means the view that the market is not just a medium of exchange but a medium of consent. Markets confer decisive legitimacy: whatever happens in a market reflects the will of the people. So, if a corporation enjoys a monopoly it is because people want it to. According to market populists, democratically elected governments are therefore behaving undemocratically when they seek to curb the monopoly power of giant corporations.

But if the market is indeed a real-life utopia, what kind of utopia is it? In his book on utopianism, Kumar distinguishes four types of utopia (1991: 18–19):

- *Cockaigne*: the land of abundance, enjoyment and pleasure.
- *Paradise*: a golden age, in which people live simply and in harmony with nature.
- *The millennium*: the hope of a new world order under the guidance of God.
- *The ideal city*: the good society designed by a rational plan. Kumar remarks that 'Architecture has always been the most utopian of all the arts' (p. 14).

In this framework, the market comes closest to the first category, the materially prosperous and hedonistic land of Cockaigne. The crucial difference is that, unlike Cockaigne, we have to work in order to enjoy prosperity.

Interestingly, as far as utopians are concerned Cockaigne is the least popular of the four. To them it is a fool's paradise, a child's or a poor person's vision of heaven as an escape from toil and suffering. In this mythical land houses are made of barley sugar and cake, the rivers flow with wine, and fish leap helpfully out on to the bank and offer themselves as food.

Kumar argues that Cockaigne cannot stand as a realized project because it would implode into a self-destructive orgy of insatiable desire (1991: 18) – a theme traceable in sociological thought to Durkheim's concept of anomie, the absence of norms that govern behaviour and set standards by which satisfaction and dissatisfaction can be gauged.

The suspicion that material affluence is hollow derives from a profound cultural unease, perhaps a legacy of the Protestant ethic and the feelings of guilt it provokes. By way of illustration, we may consider our reactions to people who retire abroad to cheaper and sunnier places. For British readers, the paradigm case is the Costa del Sol in Andalucía. British myths about such migrants are ambivalent. On the one hand, we may envy them for having found a promised land of ease, comfort and contentment: if not Cockaigne then Eldorado. On the other hand, we may pity and despise them for being a desperate enclave, exiled from their homeland, unwilling and unable to integrate into the host society, pathetically reliant on satellite television and trips to Gibraltar, given over to the temporary gratifications of alcohol, drugs and promiscuity, and facing an uncertain fate as they grow old, frail and dependent. Karen O'Reilly's (2000) fieldwork among this expatriate community shows that the stereotypes reflect our own ambivalence rather than the social reality of Andalucían life.

Unlike the other kinds of utopia, Cockaigne does not require us to become different people. We stay the same – mere consumers – but our material circumstances improve. Cockaigne provides no role for utopian visionaries. Since utopians want new people in their ideal societies, they reject Cockaigne as vulgar materialism. In their eyes, Cockaigne panders to consumerism rather than educating us to reject it.

From an anthropological perspective, not just Cockaigne but 'the market' is a myth. The social world has *markets*, not 'the market'. 'The market' doubly misrepresents social reality (Eriksen 1995: 177–8). First, it confers on its Western champions the power to name other people's trading activities. *We* in the West have 'the market', *they* – the Third World, the socialists and communists, the primitive societies – have less rational forms of exchange. Second, it subsumes under one hegemonic concept all the diverse trading activities that take place in Western capitalism. Davis distinguishes forty-two different forms of exchange in British culture, each with its own norms of conduct:

alms-giving, altruism, arbitrage, banking, barter, bribery, burglary, buying/selling, charity, commodity-dealing, corruption, donation, employment, exploitation, expropriation, extortion, futures trading, giving, huckstering, insider dealing, insurance, marketing, money-lending, mortgaging, mugging, pawning, profiteering, prostitution, reciprocity, renting, retailing, robbery, scrounging, shoplifting, shopping, simony, social wage, swapping, theft, tipping, trading, and wholesaling. (Davis 1992: 29)

As argued earlier, 'the market' is a compound of description, analysis and prescription. 'The market' as myth cuts itself free from the descriptive element, and therefore from the social reality of markets. 'The market' fuses analysis and prescription, producing a reified ideal of the 'free' market characterized by 'perfect' competition. Departures from the ideal are called market 'distortions' or 'imperfections'. Often they are attributed to 'externalities' that damage the market. 'The market' is a sacred ideal protected from contamination by the profane world. Market failure comes to mean the converse of what we might suppose. The market has not failed us, we have failed the market.

Contained within the utopian vision of free market consumer society are, so critics say, social forces that lead straight to dystopia. The following sections discuss four of these forces: conspicuous consumption, individualism, narcissism and fetishism.

Conspicuous consumption

The *potlatch* (a Chinook word) is a sumptuous gift-giving ceremony which expresses and reinforces social hierarchy. The donor demonstrates his wealth by distributing lavish gifts, while the recipients symbolically acknowledge their social inferiority by accepting gifts whose value they cannot match in return. Potlatches typically occur as an element in rites of passage such as weddings.

Potlatches are competitive, expressing not just the social superiority of donor over recipients but also status rivalry between donors. The system produces a ratchet effect, as wealthy people strive to surpass one another through potlatches that become ever more extravagant. Among the

Kwakiutl, the potlatch evolved to include ostentatious destruction of wealth in front of rivals: throwing away food, setting fire to carpets and tents, even drowning slaves at sea (Eriksen 1995: 168).

In his classic work, *The Theory of the Leisure Class* (1925/1899), Thorstein Veblen drew on ethnographic studies of 'primitive' societies in order to analyse the consumption patterns of the industrial and commercial bourgeoisie of north-eastern America. These were America's new rich, the social class that had defeated the land- and slave-owners of the Old South in the Civil War of 1861–5.

The newly rich leisure class was characterized by conspicuous consumption. Its great dynasties – the Vanderbilts, Rockefellers, Rothschilds and Astors – were desperate to convert some of their wealth into social status. Various tactics were involved.

The potlatch Elegant dinners, lavish entertainments and glittering balls were a modern equivalent of the 'primitive' potlatch.

The stately mansion with its domestic servants Galbraith (1977: 61–2) cites the example of *The Breakers*, built at the turn of the century for Commodore Vanderbilt at Newport, Rhode Island, at an estimated cost of 3 million dollars. (By contrast, Vanderbilt University in Nashville cost a mere 1 million.) The great house required a huge retinue of domestic servants, whose professional obsequiousness confirmed the superiority of their masters and mistresses, thus symbolically reaffirming the class structure.

The news media Another key pleasure of the leisure class is celebrity. They like reading about themselves, and they relish the thought that lesser people are doing so too. Hence the close links between the *nouveaux riches* and newspaper proprietors, and the significance of society and gossip columns. The exhibitionism of the rich feeds the voyeurism of the poor.

Marriage The *nouveaux riches* of America had money but lacked status, the old families of Europe had status but not money. Unsurprisingly, a healthy market developed to match the heirs to American fortunes with the penniless daughters of European aristocrats. The American entrepreneurs could cast off their robber baron image, while the Europeans benefited from a much needed injection of cash.

Gambling   As well as providing a location for matchmaking, the French Riviera also offered casinos, an opulent environment for gambling. In the spirit of the potlatch, the point of gambling was not to make money but to lose it.

Conspicuous consumption entails conspicuous leisure; the leisure class must not work. Clothing was an important symbol of this. Clothes must be expensive and impractical. A gentleman's attire – patent leather shoes, frock coat, top hat, walking-stick, and irreproachable linen – proclaim the unsuitability of labour. So do the clothes of a gentlewoman, who is not a worker but a trophy.

The suitable pursuits of a gentleman are 'government, war, sports, and devout observances'. They involve effort, certainly, but not wage labour. Even when, as is the case with government and war, they generate money, 'it is gain obtained by the honourable methods of seizure and conversion' (Veblen 1925/1899: 40) – predatory, not productive. Perhaps a survival of this cult of the gentlemanly lifestyle is, or at least until recently was, the cultural preference for amateurism in sport. In England, an annual match used to be staged between the 'gentlemen', for whom cricket was an unpaid cultivated pursuit, and the 'players' who earned their living from it.

It is debatable whether Veblen's work should be seen as objective social science or as satire. Galbraith opts for the latter. For him, Veblen was engaged in a barely concealed attack on the antics of America's *nouveaux riches*. Veblen's frequent references to the cultural practices of savages were intended to be offensive to the scions of American capitalism. Papuan chiefs mutilated the face and breasts of their wives, while the Vanderbilts encased their women in corsets – which amounted to the same thing.

Whether satire or social science, Veblen's tone is condemnatory. Extravagant, ostentatious, deliberately wasteful: these people are unproductive parasites, yet they enjoy, through the power of emulation, disproportionate power in shaping public taste. They teach us, their social inferiors, to treat objects as status symbols. Instead of relying on what Veblen calls our 'instinct for workmanship', valuing well-made goods for the use they give us, we become attuned to 'pecuniary comparison', with extravagance transformed from vice to virtue. Dant draws attention to Veblen's tirade on the superiority of machine-manufactured aluminium spoons over silver spoons at a hundred times the price. It is, as Dant remarks, 'the very familiar argument of taste versus utility' (1999: 19). We shall meet it again in chapter 6, in the guise of value-for-money consumerism.

Individualism, consumerism and the decline of community

Robert Putnam (1995, 2001) captures rampant individualism in an arresting phrase: 'bowling alone'. According to him, not only are fewer Americans taking part in tenpin bowling leagues, they increasingly go bowling without any partner or opponent at all. The lone bowler is a consumer of a service, not a participant in a social activity. What is true of bowling holds good, Putnam says, for a host of other voluntary activities such as voting, churchgoing, charitable work, labour unions, and youth organizations. They are all in decline. People have retreated into the domestic sphere – and what do they do there? They spend more and more time in front of TV and computer screens rather than in personal interaction with their family.

Bowling alone is a symbol of the collapse of community, the decline of civil society and the wasting away of democracy. It signals a loss of 'social capital', by which Putnam means 'features of social organization such as networks, norms, and social trust that facilitate co-ordination and co-operation for mutual benefit' (Putnam 1995: 67). The decline began in the 1960s. Unless we can restore society's stock of social capital we face a future of failing education, ill-health and crime.

Putnam's ideas are echoed in the work of 'communitarians' such as Amitai Etzioni. The West is, as he puts it, suffering a cold season of excessive individualism, and yearns for the warmth of community to allow human relations to bloom. He agrees with Putnam that the present malaise can be traced to the cultural turmoil of the permissive 1960s, which destroyed old social institutions without replacing them with viable alternatives. Its legacy has been moral anarchy, leaving individuals bereft of social support and moral guidance. Out of this spiritual wasteland has grown the threat of authoritarian fundamentalism, a pathological response to a pathology.

Communitarians argue for a middle or 'third' way between the extremes of individualism and authoritarianism, the free market and state control. They aim to promote character virtues, restoring the moral balance between rights and responsibilities and socializing citizens into 'values that command our support because they are morally compelling' (Etzioni 1995: 24). Their project is to turn consumers back into citizens.

Francis Fukuyama, a prophet who proclaimed the triumph of capitalism and the end of history, shares these fears. In *The Great Disruption* (1999), Fukuyama repeatedly refers to the contemporary climate of individualism as 'intensive', 'excessive' and 'unbridled'. Over-emphasis on 'rights-based individualism' (Fukuyama 1995: 308) is the greatest threat to Western democracy. But like Etzioni and Putnam, he is optimistic that social capital will be rebuilt and community restored. Their ideas have been well received by politicians and policy-makers, who are attracted by the proposition that civil society can be reinvigorated, rather cheaply, by promoting self-reliance.

The corrosion of community by individualism and consumerism is a recurrent theme in Western social thought, and in empirical studies of local communities. Young and Willmott's (1962/1957) classic study of Bethnal Green in the East End of London in the 1950s is a paradigm case. Bethnal Green was presented as the model of a traditional working-class community: homogeneously working-class, intergenerationally stable, neighbourly, solidaristic, collectivist, unscarred by status striving. Mistrust of outsiders and official agencies was offset by effective mechanisms of social control in the community, by an ethic of reciprocity and mutual aid, by strong attachment to locality – even neighbouring Stepney was foreign territory – and above all by an extended kinship system in which the mother–daughter tie was crucial. In Young and Willmott's account, Bethnal Green and neighbourhoods like it were under threat from technocratic town planners who coldly destroyed communities without deigning to consult the residents.

Bethnal Green is not just a district of London, but a symbol rich in emotion. It is, as Platt observes, 'a sort of Utopia, a working-class pastoral whose simple virtues show up the coldness, falsity and inhumanity of the rest of (middle-class) society' (1971: 139). It has no place for acquisitive middle-class consumerism. In Kumar's classification of utopias, it is a paradise.

The impact of consumerism on paradise is shown in Young and Willmott's account of the lives of people who had left Bethnal Green for a new housing estate at 'Greenleigh' on the outskirts of London. Isolated from kin and estranged from neighbours, they became 'house-centred' rather than 'people-centred'. Their relations with neighbours showed a noxious mix of pride and envy, as they fought compulsively 'to keep up with the Joneses'. In Bethnal Green, the paradise, character rather than status was what counted. In 'Greenleigh', after the Fall, people were not well enough known to be judged by their character, so their status was determined by their possessions.

A similar judgement on consumerism can be found in American community studies, for example in Robert and Helen Lynd's research in 'Middletown' (Muncie, Indiana). Having first studied Muncie in 1924, the Lynds returned in 1935 to find that people had been 'hypnotized by the gorged stream of new things to buy' (Lynd and Lynd 1937: 46). Automobiles were top of their list. *Middletown in Transition* reads as a lament for the lost world of small town America.

To some European thinkers, consumerism is an infection imported from America. This theme runs through Richard Hoggart's study of working-class culture in Britain (Hoggart 1958). He celebrates what he calls 'the full rich life' of the working class, emphasizing the complex connections between public culture and private experiences. This organic culture began to decay in the 1930s; by the 1950s young people had rejected it utterly. In a chapter entitled 'The newer mass art: sex in shiny packets', Hoggart deplores the culture of 'the juke-box boys'. These vain young men 'are living to a large extent in a myth-world compounded of a few simple elements which they take to be those of American life' (Hoggart 1958: 248). They foolishly look to America because they think it is in the vanguard of progress. Even their bodies are corrupted: they imitate Humphrey Bogart, and affect what Hoggart calls 'an American slouch' (instead of standing up straight, presumably). The records they listen to are almost all American. If they read, it will be 'spicy' magazines, crime novels, thrillers and sexually explicit material. Some of this is imported from America, while the rest is pathetic British mimicry. Hoggart's judgement is categorical (1958: 270): 'This is the popular literature of an empty megalopolitan world.'

Hoggart is not crudely anti-American. He praises creative American writing about low life, citing William Faulkner's *Sanctuary* (published 1931) as an example of great literature. He admires Hemingway, but despises 'debased Hemingway'. Hoggart is not a European elitist despising America because it has no high culture. His somewhat shaky argument is that America lacks a popular cultural heritage. Its so-called popular culture is, according to him, entirely commercial.

Not all sociologists and cultural commentators agree with the diagnosis that consumerism entails unbridled individualism, the collapse of community and the decline of civil society. Two major American studies that offer more nuanced accounts are *The Lonely Crowd* and *Habits of the Heart*. As with the work of Putnam, Etzioni and Fukuyama, these two books have attracted a large audience, showing that they have tapped a widely felt anxiety.

The Lonely Crowd: a study of the changing American character by David Riesman (with Nathan Glazer and Reuel Denney) was first published in 1950. The book begins by distinguishing three types of character, each associated with a particular stage of society (Riesman et al. 1961/1950). First, the tradition-directed character. This is a pattern of conventional conformity, as in Durkheim's concept of 'mechanical solidarity'. In traditional societies, people conform to long-standing social norms based on their membership of a status group such as a caste, class or clan. Deviance from the status group's norms is punished through public shaming of the deviant. Tradition-directed societies are premodern.

Second, the inner-directed character. The socialization process implants deep-seated norms and values into individuals at an early stage of their life. These continue to govern the thoughts and actions of the adult, as a kind of internal 'gyroscope' that orients action towards culturally approved goals. Social control is achieved not publicly through shame but inwardly through guilt, the prompting of conscience.

Third, the other-directed character. Here, individuals are governed not by a 'gyroscope' attuned to internalized values but by a 'radar system' that monitors the behaviour of other people and seeks to align the individual with it. Conformity is achieved neither through shame nor guilt, but through anxiety.

Riesman has often been read as follows. Since tradition-directed characters are fitted only to premodern social formations such as feudalism, the choice for the modern world is between inner-directed gyroscope and other-directed radar. Increasingly, other-direction is coming to predominate. Social life and human character are thereby impoverished. Other-direction is the orientation of Whyte's 'organization man', who identifies with the aims of the corporation (Whyte 1960). His dominant anxiety is to please by fitting in: he is plastic. He lives in the suburbs, where he timidly practises 'inconspicuous consumption', seeking to blend in with the tastes of his neighbours, not compete with them. His wife colludes with him in this dystopia. Paradoxically, although they are other-directed they are not really *interested* in other people. Theirs is a life of anxious conformity and forlorn contentment masquerading as happiness.

Other-direction apparently makes a sorry contrast with inner-direction. Inner-directed people have moral fibre. They have convictions and will stand up for principles. They cultivate character virtues in themselves and their children. They are rugged individuals, but unlike their other-directed counterparts they are more likely to engage in public affairs and are capable of a genuine interest in other people. The American republic was founded on these virtues. On this reading of Riesman, the Protestant ethic that inspired the Pilgrims has given way to the anxiety-ridden conformism of the modern consumer.

Reflecting on the way his ideas had been interpreted, Riesman remarked in the preface to the 1960 edition of *The Lonely Crowd*: 'the great majority of readers in the last ten years have decided that it was better to be an inner-directed cowboy than an other-directed advertising man' (Riesman et al. 1961/1950: xvii–xviii). Yet Riesman was not aiming to praise inner-direction as necessarily virtuous. It has a dark side. Inner-directed people have had values implanted in them by their socialization. Society, as Durkheim would have reminded us, is the source of their gyroscope. Why should we admire the inner-directed person's neurotic, obsessive, guilt-ridden compliance with the dictates of a socially constructed superego? The noble Pilgrims were inner-directed, but so too are white supremacists (Riesman 1961: 434n). As for other-direction, is it so desperate? Compared to the inner-directed, other-directed people are less inhibited and more open-minded. They may not be heroic, but they are kind, considerate and tolerant. Perhaps other-direction is suspect because it is more 'feminine'. Yet, as Riesman remarks, people brought up in an oppressive puritanical milieu often respond warmly to the values of other-direction (Riesman et al. 1961/1950: xvii).

Inner- and other-direction are both types of conformity. Riesman holds up a third choice to the modern world: autonomy (Riesman et al. 1961/1950: 239–60). Autonomous people are capable of choosing whether or not to conform to social norms. They are neither maladjusted nor adjusted, but free.

To achieve autonomy in an inner-directed culture requires strength of character to resist the force of community pressure and the freight of internalized values. For Riesman, though, the barriers to achieving autonomy in an other-directed culture are even more subtle and insidious. Peer group pressure and mass media indoctrination make it hard to know what one really wants. Self-consciousness may be acute, but it does not bring self-knowledge.

In the world of work, one barrier to autonomy is 'false personalization', 'the spurious and effortful glad hand'

(Riesman et al. 1961/1950: 264). Autonomy may depend on the depersonalization of work, so that it becomes less emotionally strenuous. Surprisingly, automation and bureaucracy become conditions of our freedom. Riesman later came to realize that he had been over-optimistic that autonomy could be sacrificed at work but achieved through leisure. His reconsideration is a challenge to any social philosophy that accepts unfreedom in production as a condition of freedom in consumption: 'In fact, we soon realized that the burden put on leisure by the disintegration of work is too huge to be coped with: leisure itself cannot rescue work, but fails with it, and can only be meaningful for most men if work is meaningful, so that the very qualities we looked for in leisure are more likely to come into being there if social and political action fight the two-front battle of work-and-leisure' (Riesman 1961: 456).

In 1975, twenty-five years after Riesman's book, five sociologists – Robert Bellah, Richard Madsen, William Sullivan, Ann Swidler and Steven Tipton – published the first edition of *Habits of the Heart*, subtitled *Individualism and commitment in American life* (Bellah et al. 1996).

Democracy in America is based on a constitutional system of checks and balances between institutions: the President, Congress, the judiciary, the press, the federal government and the states. The health of the political order requires that no one of these should achieve dominance over the others. The same, say Bellah et al., holds true of the cultural system. Individualism, as de Tocqueville saw, values independence and self-reliance above all other virtues. For Bellah et al., individualism has been sustainable as a force in society only because it has been enriched and held in check by two sets of values: the republican tradition and the biblical tradition. The republican tradition, derived from ancient Greece and Rome, holds that citizens are motivated not just by self-interest but also by civic virtue. Participating in public affairs entails a moral engagement with issues of justice and the public good. The biblical tradition is carried by Jewish and Christian religious communities. It teaches us to be concerned for social justice, and upholds the intrinsic worth of individuals as created by God. In the USA, the republican and biblical traditions have tended to form an alliance. Both traditions recognize a social dimension to human individuality that gives a moral foundation and purpose to public life.

American individualism has deep roots. A core belief, the heart of the American dream, is that 'economic success or misfortune is the individual's responsibility, and his or hers alone' (Bellah et al. 1996: viii). Individualism has two modes: utilitarian individualism stresses self-interest as the motive of human actions, expressive individualism emphasizes the individual's feelings and intuitions.

Bellah et al. argue that the greatest danger in contemporary America is the ascendancy of 'a strident and ultimately destructive individualism' (Bellah et al. 1996: x). They write of the discontent of a life devoted simply to personal ambition and consumerism. The language of individualism makes it hard to articulate the range and subtlety of people's aspirations.

Yet their analysis is not dystopian. The quest for self-actualization is not necessarily incompatible with a desire for deep social relationships with others. One example is in the field of religion. Another is romantic love, which may be self-indulgent but may also testify to the poverty of the isolated self and our longing for communion. Often there is a dangerous gulf between public and private life: 'Many of those with whom we talked were locked into a split between a public world of competitive striving and a private world supposed to provide the meaning and love that make competitive striving bearable' (Bellah et al. 1996: 292).

'Consumerism' too is deeply ambivalent. The creation of a consumption-oriented lifestyle can involve giving to others, or can collapse inward into a doomed defence against risk and meaninglessness. Bellah et al. distinguish between *communities* and *lifestyle enclaves*. Community is used in a strong sense to mean a group of people who are socially interdependent, participating in *practices* that are viewed as ends in themselves. A community has a history and a collective memory. It is defined by its practices, which involve commitments that transcend the individual. A university, for example, is (or was) a community devoted to such practices as teaching, learning, scholarship, research, the pursuit of knowledge, and the cultivation of sensibility and discernment. In contrast, a lifestyle enclave is a group of people who have some private consumption tastes that they share in the company of others – in a golf club, for example, or more widely in a residential suburb. A lifestyle 'celebrates the narcissism of similarity' (Bellah et al. 1996: 72). Lifestyle enclaves are segmental: they involve only a part of the individual's life, and they include only people with a common lifestyle. They are often fragile and shallow, though they may be all we have.

The culture of narcissism

When Sigmund Freud began practising psychoanalysis in the Vienna of the late nineteenth and early twentieth centuries, his bourgeois clients presented him with symptoms that he diagnosed as hysteria and obsessional neurosis. These conditions, according to Lasch (1991/1977: 41–2), were characteristic of an earlier phase of capitalist culture, in which people were slaves to the Protestant work ethic and sexuality was fiercely repressed. Contemporary culture is consumerist and sexually permissive, a combination that produces its own problem: narcissism.

In Greek mythology, Narcissus was a beautiful young man who became obsessed with his own reflection in a pool. In frustration and despair, he committed suicide. A white flower sprang up where he fell and was named after him: *narcissus*, the daffodil. Sigmund Freud took this myth and interpreted it as an expression of pathological personality development.

Love is narcissistic when we fall in love with our self projected on to someone (or something) else. Narcissists are incapable of loving another person, and refuse to be loved themselves. Not only are they vain, they are alone, since they are infatuated with a mere reflection. They may be self-absorbed, but instead of engaging in serious introspection and self-examination they seek quick fixes and easy answers – through physical exercise, or health foods, or special diets. These quasi-therapies involve not self-discovery but self-evasion, underpinned by a dread of ageing and death (Craib

1989: 108–9). Narcissists' self-obsession means that their spiritual life is impoverished and their social relationships vestigial and empty. They need our admiration and approval but cannot tolerate our friendship and love. Lasch describes their condition as marked by 'a certain protective shallowness, a fear of binding commitments, a willingness to pull up roots whenever the need arose, a desire to keep one's options open, a dislike of depending on anyone, and incapacity for loyalty or gratitude' (1991/1977: 239). Ironically, these may have become exactly the qualities needed for worldly success. Narcissistic personalities are promoted to positions of power, from where they encourage narcissistic traits in those below them.

What are the causes of the culture of narcissism? Lasch's deeply pessimistic analysis identifies a number of trends. The dominance of the mass media means the sacrifice of truth to plausibility: all that matters is that the masses swallow what they are fed. The rise of advertising promotes consumerism as a way of life, and stimulates desires that leave us perpetually unfulfilled. The decline of the family, and of all forms of organic community, disrupts the transmission of culture from generation to generation. Outdated skills and old-fashioned lifestyles: this is all that parents have to pass on to their children. The legacy is useless, and children reject it. Parent–child relationships therefore become shallow (Craib 1989: 111). As the authority of the family wanes, so we are delivered into the custody of corporate bureaucracies, where career advancement and even survival demand that we become preoccupied with impression management.

Narcissism is not just a feature of interpersonal relations. Modern life breeds a narcissistic relationship to material objects, as Minsky argues. 'Goods' – a word she invariably puts in inverted commas, to remind us that we are infatuated – are symbolic items 'which represent longed-for aspects of ourselves that we unconsciously imagine we can acquire from the external world' (Minsky 1998: 185). Consuming 'goods', viewed psychoanalytically, is connected to the baby's experience of consuming the mother for psychic as well as physical survival. The pleasures of consumption symbolize our infant experience of the 'good breast' in the oral stage of sexuality. Consuming 'goods' is an act of psychic survival. Retail therapy – shop till you drop – provides a feeling of satiation, as when a baby has a good feed at the mother's breast. In adult life, such feelings are destined to be fleeting and fragile. Worse, they are destructive. Contemporary rates of consumption are the outcome not only of the desire for a higher standard of living, but the need to satisfy infantile forms of identity. Capitalism is sucking Mother Earth dry.

If this psychoanalytic approach seems fanciful, consider the irrational appeal of spotlessly new consumer 'goods'. Narcissistic love explains their allure. Car manufacturers know this: new cars must be gleaming, and must exude the 'new car smell' – the automobile equivalent of a perfume from Paris. Even something as apparently banal as a new refrigerator 'reflects back to us a transformed, pristine, immaculate self ready to embark on a new life' (Minsky 1998: 191). Hence the deep disillusionment the minute it gets scratched or some ornamental piece of trim falls off it. We are not merely dissatisfied customers, we are rejected lovers. The 'good' has shown itself to be 'bad'.

The pathological pursuit of pleasure through consumption of 'goods' is a regressive flight from reality, a refusal to acknowledge loss, frustration, uncertainty, ambivalence and contradiction. What Freud called the reality principle is sacrificed to the pleasure principle. We are caught up in 'manufactured fantasies of total gratification' (Lasch 1991/1977: 231). Consumption provides escapist and narcissistic forms of identity; it offers infantile gratification in place of emotional maturity. The car is often recognized as a phallic symbol, but it also represents an attempted flight back into 'the comfort, security and containment associated with the womb' (Minsky 1998: 188). These unconscious meanings are one barrier to adopting other modes of transport.

Narcissism also explains, according to Minsky, the West's treatment of the Third World. The West displays 'a narcissistic short-sightedness characterized by greed, denial and projection' (Minsky 1998: 206). Former colonial powers bolster their own failing sense of national identity through the myth of the colony's infantile dependence. Narcissism explains the policy of tied aid and the encouragement of cash crops. Psychologically, Western powers have never granted independence to their former colonies.

Narcissism should not be mistaken for confident individualism. It is not robust but impulsive and anxious. It springs from self-loathing – Narcissus, we should remember, killed himself. In Lowenthal's phrase (cited by Slater 1997: 122), mass consumer culture is 'psychoanalysis in reverse'. It does not cure neuroses but creates and intensifies them. And in place of therapy it substitutes mere commodities.

If there is no salvation through commodities, what about therapy? Since he draws so deeply on psychoanalytic concepts, surely Lasch sees psychotherapy as the treatment for narcissism? Surprisingly, as Giddens points out (1991: 179–80), he shows himself unsympathetic to psychotherapy. Lasch's concern is twofold. The first danger is infantile dependence on the therapist as expert. Psychotherapy's liberal mask conceals its authoritarian face. It sets out to make patients dependent. As cynics have often said, psychotherapy is the disease for which it declares itself to be the cure. Second, Lasch claims that psychotherapy's objective is to 'adjust' the individual to a pathological society. It palliates individual symptoms but leaves their social causes untouched. Far from advocating psychotherapy, Lasch's book ends with a plea that we demand less of life and more of ourselves (1991/1977: 248). This 'moral realism' is to be nurtured not on the psychoanalyst's couch but through 'the homely comforts of love, work, and family life'.

Commodity fetishism

'Fetishism' is derived from the pidgin *fetisso*, a term used by Portuguese slave traders operating on the Gold Coast of Africa. *Fetisso* referred to the supposedly irrational religions of the slaves, who attributed spiritual power to mere artefacts. In psychology, fetishism has been used to mean an erotic fixation on particular objects, such as shoes or aprons, or on materials such as plastics and rubber, which act as sources of sexual arousal.

When Karl Marx wrote of *commodity* fetishism in volume 1 of *Capital*, he was diagnosing a deep pathological displacement at the core of capitalism. For Marx, the real value

of a commodity is determined by the labour power that produced it. The price that commodities command in the market
is an illusion. Price does not reflect the value of labour and
therefore obscures the social relations of production. This
leads to a double distortion: commodities are treated as
if they were persons possessing agency, while persons are
reduced to commodities bought and sold merely for their
labour power. Commodity fetishism involves alienation: we
create material objects that take on a life of their own, escaping our control and shaping our lives. Real human relations
are mystified as relations between material objects. A society that fetishizes commodities is one that stultifies human
sociality.

In all these uses of the term, fetishism is diagnosed as a
pathology. It is contrasted with the real, healthy situation:
for the slavers, primitive spirits as against the true God; for
Freud, an object or part of the body, not a whole human
being; for Marx, the product instead of the true value of
the labour embodied in it. Some cultural critics argue that
fetishism characterizes most forms of thought in capitalist
societies.

One reason why shopping is so often seen as a trivial activity and a banal object of enquiry is the accusation of commodity fetishism (Miller 1998: 128). Critics tend to see the
purchase of material goods as a substitute for authentic social
relations. Just as religion is misdirected devotion to non-
existent gods, so the fetishism of commodities is a pathological mutation of human sociality into a fixation on inanimate
objects.

Following Eagleton (1991: 85), we can identify three
ideological consequences of commodity fetishism. First, a
fetishistic focus on commodities obscures the social relations
of production that produced them. In Lee's words, 'The
sphere of production is thus the night-time of the commodity: the mysterious economic dark side of social exploitation
which is so effectively concealed in the dazzling glare of the
market-place' (1993: 15). A powerful statement of this idea
is Roland Barthes's analysis of the launch of the Citroën DS
at the 1955 Paris Motor Show. He argues that the modern
automobile is 'the exact equivalent of the great Gothic cathedrals: I mean the supreme creation of an era, conceived with

passion by unknown artists, and consumed in image if not in usage by a whole population which appropriates them as a purely magical object' (Barthes 1972/1957: 88). The DS – the Déesse, or Goddess – was a luxurious car with advanced engineering and avant-garde design. Worshippers, whether in cathedrals or cars, forget the alienated human labour that built them. Similarly, Naomi Klein's *No Logo* (2000) is a statement of the power of First World brands to conceal Third World sweatshops.

Second, society becomes fragmented. The collective activity of labour is transmuted into relations between discrete material objects. The prospect of political critique recedes as it becomes harder to grasp capitalism as a totality. This is a key theme in Benjamin, as Slater emphasizes. Modernity turns us into consumers of random isolated events, and of fetishized commodities that are 'experienced through a predominantly aesthetic mode as surface or appearance without depth or historicity' (Slater 1997: 114). For Benjamin, the theorist's task is to penetrate the flux of consumerism in order to reveal the unchanging reality of capitalism. His project is 'the attempt to see, against the grain of commodity fetishism, the totality of capitalist social relations as they are filtered through each of its commodified fragments' (Slater 1997: 115).

Third, the dominant role of commodities means that human culture, a social creation, comes to appear as natural and inevitable. Adorno warned against this in his concept of 'identity thinking'. In Slater's words: 'Consumer culture promotes the false sense that subject and object, individual and consumer good, audience and culture perfectly match and are reconciled now, under present social conditions' (1997: 122).

This is an important element in Barthes's analysis of mythologies. Successful ideologies render their beliefs natural and self-evident, creating as tight a fit as possible between themselves and social reality so as to snuff out any possibility of critique. Ideologies present themselves as hard-bitten realism: this is the way the world is. Advocates of 'the market' typically adopt this line, as in the Thatcherite slogan, 'there is no alternative'. Ruling ideologies do not necessarily combat alternative ideas, but try to suppress them by making them unthinkable.

For Marx, mystification is essential to the capitalist system. It is not just that we are all victims of a shared delusion about commodities. Rather, as Eagleton points out, 'Marx is not claiming that under capitalism commodities *appear* to exercise a tyrannical sway over social relations; he is arguing that they actually do' (1991: 85). Capitalism depends on a dislocation between appearance and reality, and we cannot overthrow it merely by changing our perceptions.

One way to read Marx is as a romantic who celebrated the authenticity of a society based on craft production and governed by use-value – a society in which production and consumption were organically linked. Marx sees use-value as necessarily related to human needs; but are needs simply given in nature (Dant 1999: 46)? Surely, as Baudrillard argues (1981), needs and use-values are themselves socially constructed? Perhaps Marx succumbed to the dominant ideology of the nineteenth century, which idealized work, rationality and utility (Lee 1993: 22). In his critique of the fetishism of commodities, Marx is accused by his critics of fetishizing use-value.

Mass society, mass culture?

If the free market is the dominant contemporary assertion of utopia, mass society is the most powerful dystopia. Mass society is the free market through the looking-glass, illustrating Carey's remark that 'a dystopia is merely a utopia from another point of view' (1999: xii).

The theory of mass society was most powerfully stated by members of the Frankfurt School, notably Theodor Adorno, Max Horkheimer and Herbert Marcuse. Their strategy is to mount an 'immanent critique' of capitalism, judging it by its own claims and demonstrating their inherent contradictions.

Taking the themes I have identified above (pp. 56–7) as defining the market, we can represent the contrast with mass society as in the box overleaf. Listed in the first column are the claims of the market to be the fulfilment of Enlightenment rationalism. The second column shows the results of an immanent critique of these pretensions, as follows.

The market	Mass society
Individualism	Atomization
Instrumental rationality	Dehumanization
Efficiency	Exploitation
Freedom	Social control
Choice	Pseudo-individualization
Prosperity	Commodity fetishism
Dynamism	Diachronic standardization
Consumption	Consumerism

Atomization   The ascendancy of individualism brings the collapse of organic communities and civil society. Atomized societies breed positivist social science: technically hypertrophied, intellectually bankrupt, capable only of conducting banal social surveys. Critical theory itself has to struggle to avoid being commodified.

Atomized societies are not merely a cause for intellectuals to lament a world we have lost; they are the breeding ground for fascism. Dictators need masses, and masses can be induced to feel a need for dictators.

Dehumanization   Commodity fetishism involves reification: people, social institutions and cultural products are turned into things. The capitalist system comes across as a massive fact. People are stupefied, infantilized and duped into acquiescence. Horkheimer and Adorno's critique is dialectical, exposing the irrationality of rationalism.

Exploitation   Although the members of the Frankfurt School focused on bourgeois culture rather than capitalist economics, they did not abandon Marx's analysis of exploitation. On the contrary, they argued that the cultural dominance of exchange-value is the key mechanism through which exploitation is concealed.

Social control Far from being a realm of freedom, mass society breeds cultural conformity and the narcosis of creativity. The Enlightenment project to gain mastery over nature leads to the manipulative control of human beings. Hence 'the domination of nature and social domination are mutually implicated' (Delanty 1999: 23).

Pseudo-individualization The market supposedly delivers a wide range of choice, while in fact offering superficial differences between standardized products. 'Badge engineering' of cars is an example of pseudo-individualization. The pioneer was Albert Sloan at General Motors in the 1920s. At the time of writing, the Volkswagen group manufactures the Audi A3, Volkswagen Golf, Seat León and Škoda Octavia – four cars with a high proportion of shared components. To its economically minded shareholders, the Volkswagen group signals the profitable economies of scale this entails. To its culturally attuned customers, Volkswagen presents four separate companies with unique models displayed in different showrooms. Each car is marketed as possessing distinctive qualities: German luxury, German quality, Spanish flair, Czech value for money.

Barthes made the same point is his analysis of the phoney war between Persil (a soap powder) and Omo (a detergent). After an elaborate analysis of the mythological differences between Persil and Omo comes the conclusion: 'There is one plane on which *Persil* and *Omo* are one and the same: the plane of the Anglo-Dutch trust *Unilever*' (Barthes 1972/1957: 40).

For the Frankfurt School, commercialized popular music is an important example of pseudo-individualization. It is a reactionary force: manufactured, self-referential and formulaic. Its impact on consumers is to induce stupefied adjustment to capitalism.

Commodity fetishism The theory of commodity fetishism, discussed above (pp. 78–81), was central to the Frankfurt School's analysis of mass society. Money dominates social relations. Adorno believed that people who buy a ticket to a concert performed by a virtuoso and conducted by a maestro are really worshipping the money they paid for it. The value of any good or activity is confirmed by its high price. An 'exclusive' perfume is therefore precisely that: poorer people are not meant to be able to afford it.

Diachronic standardization The market gives the appearance of dynamism, but the reality is stasis (Gendron 1986; Strinati 1995: 70–4). Just as pseudo-individualization hides the similarity of competing products at any given time (synchronic standardization), so too the pace of technical and cultural innovation is exaggerated, and history is denied in the onward rush of pseudo-innovation.

Consumerism As discussed in chapter 1, consumerism is used by cultural critics as a deeply pejorative term. Consumerism, in the title of Miles's (1998) book, is a way of life. It falls well short of the good life. Bocock puts it acidly: consumerism is 'the active ideology that the meaning of life is to be found in buying things and pre-packaged experiences' (1993: 48).

For the Frankfurt School, a defining characteristic of consumers is their passivity. It marks the contrast between high and mass culture. High culture has active knowledgeable connoisseurs, mass culture has passive consumers. In the classification proposed in figure 1.1 above (p. 16), the consumer is not a victim so much as a dupe. The Frankfurt School was scarcely offering a value for money critique of the market economy, nor suggesting that capitalism produces unreliable, shoddy goods. Quite the reverse, since capitalism legitimizes itself by the quality of its products. When the Berlin Wall was destroyed, East Germans gladly abandoned their Trabants for Volkswagens, as Westerners were quick to note. Capitalism's consumers are, as Bauman says, *seduced*. This recurrent theme links to the Frankfurt School's pessimism, epitomized in Marcuse's *One Dimensional Man* (1964). The revolutionary overthrow of the capitalist system is not to be accomplished by an atomized mass of satiated consumers.

Horkheimer and Adorno abandoned the terms 'mass society' and 'mass culture' in favour of one they coined themselves: 'the culture industry'. In doing so they avoided the implication that mass culture arises spontaneously from the masses; rather, it is imposed. Their phrase was meant to be provocative. In German intellectual thought, as Callinicos remarks (1999: 253), it is a contradiction in terms. Authentic cultural products cannot be produced industrially, but demand the genius of the creative artist. The culture industry, in contrast, is capable only of products that are standardized and predictable. The culture industry actively produces the passive consumer.

4
Living in Consumer Society

Pierre Bourdieu: manoeuvres in the field of consumption

'Taste classifies, and it classifies the classifier' (Bourdieu 1984: 6). As consumers we make choices, but paradoxically we create our unfreedom in the very act of choosing. However hotly we may deny it, we classify ourselves through our tastes.

Bourdieu's *Distinction* begins with a critique of Kant's notion that the true appreciation of art forms is 'disinterested'. Aesthetic appreciation, Kant insists, is not to be confused with morality or pleasure. Contrary to Kant, Bourdieu argues that there is no such thing as a pure appreciation of the arts. Taste is never disinterested; there are always vested interests. For example, a successful ploy of cultural elites is to claim as natural endowments tastes that were in fact acquired through socialization in the family and at school. As Bourdieu says, 'The ideology of natural taste owes its plausibility and its efficacy to the fact that, like all the ideological strategies generated in the everyday class struggle, it *naturalizes* real differences, converting differences in the mode of acquisition of culture into differences of nature' (1984: 68). The bourgeoisie have the power successfully to disguise what they have learned as what they were born with.

They acquire tastes which they then pretend came naturally. The rest of society is meant to defer to the bourgeoisie because of their superiority of personal character.

Disinterestedness is culturally enshrined as *the* way to view works of art. It legitimates the power of the dominant stratum in society, the bourgeoisie. Only people who enjoy a life of ease, and who have received an elite education, can afford the luxury of art for art's sake. To everyone else it is at best unfathomable and at worst repulsive, epitomized by abstract paintings that represent nothing, music without tunes or rhythm, and novels with no characters and no plot.

'Legitimate taste' stands at the top of a three-tiered hierarchy of taste. Immediately below it is 'middle-brow' taste, which prefers minor works of major arts (for example, musicals and light opera) or major works of the minor arts (for example, photography).

At the bottom of the hierarchy is 'popular' taste. Here Bourdieu writes of 'the choice of the necessary' (1984: 372–96). Unable to share in or even to imitate the supposed disinterestedness of legitimate taste, popular taste is oriented to pleasure. Paintings must represent nice things and attractive people, music must be tuneful, novels must tell a story. Similarly, photography means capturing happy scenes of family life. Along with pleasure goes utility and function. Legitimate taste, in contrast, turns everything into a question of aesthetics. Thus designer chairs become cultural icons, and the uncomfortable products of the Bauhaus are perversely preferred to the cosy armchair. For popular taste, an uncomfortable chair is completely pointless. Morality is also involved. In his home town of Eastwood in Nottinghamshire, D. H. Lawrence was until recently remembered less as a great novelist than as the man who wrote *Lady Chatterley's Lover*, an obscene piece of pornography that deserved to be banned. (International interest in Lawrence has grown. Eastwood has seen a market opportunity, and now adopts a more positive evaluation of the man and his work.)

Art for art's sake tends to be scandalous to popular taste. This points to a crucial defect in Veblen's approach. His theory, as has often been pointed out, rests on the assumption that social inferiors will inevitably try to emulate their 'betters'. Bourdieu, in contrast, points to the opposite effect:

distaste at the behaviour of the powerful. Their cultural practices are 'not for us'. Taste implies distaste; and what we dislike is just as important as what we like. Bourdieu is fond of quoting an epigram of La Rochefoucauld: 'Our pride is more offended by attacks on our tastes than on our opinions.' Taste involves what Bourdieu calls 'symbolic violence', acts of humiliation and degradation through which the social hierarchy is reinforced.

Bourdieu argues that tastes in different fields tend to be *homologous*. This means that all the choices we make in apparently different fields of social life – the books we read, the music we listen to, the food we eat, our holiday destinations, the friendships and partnerships we form, our religious affiliations and so on – have underlying similarities. Suppose we know that someone is a devotee of Western classical music, attends concerts regularly and has a large collection of compact discs drawn exclusively from the classical repertoire. Given such tastes in music, how likely is it that this person will read Westerns, eat TexMex, take holidays in Benidorm, be married to a coal miner, or be a member of the Moonies? While we should avoid crude stereotyping, it would be foolish to deny that people's lifestyles have a certain coherence. Our tastes in different fields are not simply random, but structured.

The structuring principle is what Bourdieu calls *habitus*. The habitus is a set of intellectual and emotional dispositions, typically acquired during our formative years through the family and the education system. Through habitus the class structure is reproduced from one generation to the next.

Bourdieu's critics accuse him of being a determinist who fails to acknowledge the scope for the exercise of our free will. Surely we are not total conformists shaped by our socialization? Many intellectuals are not snobbish, just as many manual workers are highly learned. Even the derided petty bourgeois middlebrows may be less constricted in their tastes than their despisers believe.

According to Alexander (1995: 136), habitus is 'a Trojan horse for determinism', and therefore a gift we should return to sender. Similarly, Mouzelis (1995) argues that Bourdieu pays too little attention to consciously developed tastes, and to our ability to reflect on and break free from the socialization we have received. In his own defence, Bourdieu emphatically denies that he is a determinist. What he rejects is the facile optimism that personal transformation and social change are easily accomplished. He comments wryly on the tendency of leftist intellectuals to oscillate between lionizing the working class as the agents of the revolution, and despairing of their willingness to succumb to the lure of capitalist consumerism.

Returning to Bourdieu's aphorism – 'taste classifies, and it classifies the classifier' – does it imply that there is no escape from the grid of social classification? Is it possible to break free from the matrix of consumer society?

Semiotic democracy: competent subversion

One view is that instead of escaping from consumption we simply need to be adept at it. On the utilitarian dimension, this is achieved through becoming a fully rational actor in a free market – a utopia explored above in chapter 3. On the expressive dimension, we find a utopia captured in Fiske's phrase, 'semiotic democracy'.

Drawing on the work of de Certeau (1984), Fiske emphasizes the extent to which consumers evade, subvert, oppose and transform the meanings that producers seek to inject into commodities. No corporation, however mighty, can force meanings on us. We use their products for our purposes. 'Popular culture', Fiske insists, 'is made by the people, not by the culture industry' (1989: 24).

The pitiful failure of the Ford Edsel is said to show the corporation's impotence. Backed by the insights of depth psychology and a multi-million dollar advertising campaign, the stylistically idiosyncratic Edsel (named after Henry Ford's only son) was launched in 1957 as the most powerful mass production automobile in the world. Sales remained stubbornly low, and the model was eventually withdrawn three years later. At the heart of its failure, it has been argued (Gartman 1994: 174–9), was consumers' recognition that the superficially wayward design concealed a banal product of the Detroit assembly lines. Consumers knew they were being duped.

Global capitalism may pursue homogeneity, but it cannot succeed. All it can do is produce a repertoire of cultural items which consumers are free to use or reject. Consumption is productive, since it necessarily involves the creation of meaning. It is also egalitarian: poor people, in fact, are often the most productive consumers, deploying tactics of resistance that are flamboyant, sophisticated and sassy (Fiske 1989: 35). Fiske's account does not allow a place for the downtrodden poor.

His conclusion is sanguine:

> If a particular commodity is to be made part of popular culture, it must offer opportunities for resisting or evasive uses or readings, and these opportunities must be accepted. The production of these is beyond the control of the producers of the financial commodity: it lies instead in the popular creativity of the users of that commodity in the cultural economy. (Fiske 1989: 32).

But is Fiske right? A few notorious failures like the Edsel, and a succession of small victories for consumer guerrillas, scarcely add up to the defeat of commodification. The dark cultural pessimism of the Frankfurt School has been replaced by a bright optimism. Fiske is so concerned to uphold the creative activity of consumers that he obliterates any distinction between mass culture and popular culture. His is a variant of the model of the consumer as chooser. While seemingly radical and liberating, his approach unintentionally aligns itself with right-wing celebration of the sovereign consumer (McGuigan 1992). Semiotic democracy is the free market in expressive mode. Both are myths.

The cultural omnivore: escape through embrace?

One way to transcend consumption, paradoxically, might be to embrace it wholeheartedly in all its manifestations. Instead of being locked into rigid commitments that classify and constrain us, we might break free of classification altogether. Peterson and Kern's concept of the cultural omnivore captures this. It takes Fiske's semiotic democracy to its ultimate egalitarian conclusion.

Peterson and Kern (1996) argue that status distinction is in decline. Tastes have broadened. We have learned to appreciate a wide variety of cultural forms, and no longer define our identity in terms of fixed allegiances to particular genres. A narrow diet has been replaced by omnivorousness, and snobbishness has yielded to an easy-going, benign cultural pluralism. To paraphrase Marx and Engels, we can listen to New Age in the morning, ballet music in the afternoon and heavy metal in the evening, without ever becoming a pagan, a balletomane or a head banger.

But is cultural omnivorousness a genuine escape? Displaying apparent command of a variety of cultural forms can itself convey the prestige associated with being 'cosmopolitan'. The supposed omnivore is usually highly selective, as Bryson (1996) points out. A classical music connoisseur may gain status by familiarity with modern jazz or avant-garde rock, but will know to avoid easy listening and Country and Western.

Cultural omnivorousness is a game for the cultural elite. To quote Bourdieu: 'The reader of the popular-science monthly *Science et Vie* who talks about the genetic code or the incest taboo exposes himself to ridicule as soon as he ventures outside the circle of his peers, whereas Claude Lévi-Strauss or Jacques Monod can only derive additional prestige from their excursions into the field of music or philosophy' (1984: 24–5). Intellectuals award themselves a licence to range freely, but deny it to self-taught seekers after knowledge.

It is perhaps naïve to see cultural omnivorousness as a means of escape from the field of consumption. Omnivorousness is a move within the game, and available only to the high status players. Status distinction may well have become subtler, less overt and not so readily detectable. If so, it is not the end of snobbery but rather, as Warde et al. say, 'a shift from invidious to insidious comparison' (1999: 123).

Citizenship and the anti-consumer: escape through virtue?

The relationship between consumerism and citizenship is problematic. One recurrent concern is that the rhetoric of 'citizenship' has become so debased that the only rights we have left are our rights as consumers. This was and is a theme in the neoliberal agenda to revolutionize the relationship between the individual, civil society and the state. The neoliberal right equates citizens and consumers. Its project is to transform all social relationships into market exchanges. The neoliberal left has stretched the concept of consumer towards the citizen by embracing socially aware consumerism, a consumerism of the long term (Gabriel and Lang 1995: 175–6). The vision of 'stakeholder capitalism' captures this desire to reconcile citizenship and consumerism.

In both its right-wing and left-wing versions, the neoliberal project cannot easily reconcile the freedom of sovereign consumers with the duties of responsible citizens. In Britain, Thatcherism took as part of its mission a drive to reform people's self-understanding, attitudes, desires, values, expectations and goals. The mission was not totally consistent, since it comprised a set of characters or role models that were not compatible with one another. Heelas (1991) brings this out very clearly. On his analysis, Thatcherism held up four such characters: the *enterprising self*, people who show drive and initiative, welcoming change and responding positively to the challenges it brings; the *sovereign consumer*, people who actively pursue their own goals in the marketplace without depending on welfare handouts from the state; the *active citizen*, those who contribute voluntarily to the well-being of the community; and the *conservative self*, holding firm 'Victorian' values transmitted through traditional schooling and the conventional nuclear family.

Heelas identifies a conflict between the sovereign consumer and the conservative self. Whenever it was forced to choose between them, Thatcherite neoliberalism upheld the conservative self. The sovereign consumer was not free to choose 'permissiveness', and educators were forbidden from 'promoting' homosexuality. Consumer sovereignty was thus constrained by the need to have conservative values.

Inheriting parts of the Thatcherite agenda, the 'New' Labour government in the UK has emphasized citizens' duties rather than their rights and liberties. It displays a striking degree of authoritarianism in, for example, its zero-tolerance policies on law and order, its hard response to asylum seekers, and its uneasily illiberal view of same-sex relationships. Like Thatcherism before it, 'new' Labour set itself up as guardian of the nation's morals (Callinicos 2001: 44–67), proclaiming values which all good citizens are required to share.

The *flâneur:* escape through artistry?

The dictionary definition of *flâneur* is unpromising: a stroller, idler, lounger, loafer. Originally a slang expression, its official recognition by the Académie Française was belatedly granted in 1879. Like its English equivalents the word is pejorative.

Out of this inauspicious material, sociologists, cultural theorists and art critics have created a rich discourse about the practice and significance of *flânerie*. The classic source is Walter Benjamin's monumental Arcades Project, which he embarked on in 1927 and which remained incomplete at his death in 1940. Benjamin was inspired by Edgar Allen Poe's enigmatic story of 1840, *The Man of the Crowd*, Charles Baudelaire's 1863 essay, *The Painter of Modern Life*, and Louis Aragon's reverie, *Paris Peasant*, of 1926. This is an outstanding example of the use of literary sources in the service of social science. Many sociologists are uneasy with it on exactly that ground. Should we rely, for a serious ethnography of Paris, on a bohemian poet (Baudelaire), a surrealist poet and novelist (Aragon), or an American writer (Poe) whose seminal story is set not in Paris but in London, a city he had never even visited?

Discourse about *flânerie* predates Benjamin. It was a staple of nineteenth-century reflection on Parisian life. Countless publications known as 'physiognomies' were sold in the 1830s and 1840s as guide books for a mass public of would-be *flâneurs*, offering stereotypes of the various 'characters' one might observe in the metropolis. One leading compendium was Victor Fournel's 1858 publication, *Ce qu'on voit dans les rues de Paris* (what one sees in the streets of Paris). Some of the century's greatest artists enacted the role of *flâneur*, notably Charles Baudelaire and Edmond de Goncourt among the writers, and Edouard Manet, Gustave Caillebotte and Edgar Degas among the impressionist painters.

Recent writing on the *flâneur* brings out a number of themes, some of them incompatible with others. The *flâneur* has been identified in varying ways:

A dandy 'The *flâneurs* were a form of dandy who devoted their lives to the social milieux of the arcades and were therefore privileged observers of social mores' (Chaney 1996: 79). The *flâneur* displayed an immaculate sartorial style: top hat, frock coat, cane or tightly rolled umbrella, newspaper, cigar. A precursor of the Parisian *flâneur* was the eighteenth-century English dandy, a social type pioneered by Beau Brummell. Elegant attire was a means to conceal social origins and identity. The British Prime Minister, Benjamin Disraeli, used dandyism to deflect attention from the social stigma of his Jewish background (Chaney 1996: 152). Like the dandy, the *flâneur* parades his sartorial surface precisely in order *not* to be penetrated by the observer's gaze.

A window-shopper Baron Haussmann's rebuilding of Paris from 1853 to 1870 under Louis Napoleon's Second Empire created a modern city of boulevards which were suitable, according to Bocock, 'for flâneurs to stroll along, to display their clothes and to window shop' (1993: 16).

A playful stroller 'The *flâneur* is a playful and transgressive figure' who strolls through the urban scene dispassionately gazing at the commodities on display (Miles 1998: 67). This postmodern take on the *flâneur* opens up the possibility that *flânerie* continues to flourish in the post-industrial cities of the late twentieth and early twenty-first centuries.

An exhibitionist and voyeur The *flâneur*'s 'purpose in window shopping and displaying stylish purchases, including clothing, was nothing more than to see and be seen. The *flâneur* illustrates the intense processes of voyeurism and exhibitionism that for Benjamin characterized many of the major cities at the turn of the century' (Edwards 2000: 22).

A sexual prospector In his account of his life in Paris in the 1980s and 1990s, Edmund White tells of his own *flânerie*: cruising the Tuileries and the Palais Royal in search of same-sex encounters. It is a contemporary version of an original theme in *flânerie*.

In Paris in the 1860s there were some 35,000 registered prostitutes for a population of around 1 million. The abundant supply indicates a high level of demand. Among the prostitutes' clients were *flâneurs*: mock-chivalrous predators on working-class women (Smith 1995: 33–57). For example, in *A Bar at the Folies-Bergère* Manet paints a startling contrast between the reflection of the barmaid in the mirror, showing an attentive young woman leaning forward invitingly towards her client, and the same barmaid staring out of the picture with a gaze of inner desolation. The reality and the appearance of emotional labour are contrasted in the image and its reflection. The barmaid offers both alcohol and herself; in the ironic phrase of the time, she is a seller of consolation. She knows the *flâneur* is not a sentimental Victorian rescuer of fallen women.

A misanthrope The predatory *flâneur* may be a misanthrope. His detached irony easily mutates into contempt for common humanity, as it did for Degas, who ended life as an embittered, anti-Semitic recluse.

An amateur detective When the *flâneur* strolls through the cityscape his attention is drawn not by obvious incidents apparent to anyone, but by singular, arcane, fleeting impressions that capture delectable features of the human comedy. Newspapers are among the *flâneur*'s indispensable accessories. He reads them less for their reports of the affairs of state than for the personal notices and the gossip. Conan Doyle's fictional Sherlock Holmes did exactly that. So did the novelist Marcel Proust. As his contemporary Lucien Daudet wrote of him: 'He read newspapers with great care. He wouldn't even overlook the news-in-brief section. A news-in-brief told by him turned into a whole tragic or comic novel, thanks to his imagination and his fantasy' (quoted in de Botton 1998: 38). This alertness to the unconsidered fragments of contemporary life is suggested by the description of the *flâneur* as a ragpicker. The amateur detective's creative capacity is similarly linked to the conception of the *flâneur* as visionary artist.

As well as these various way of characterizing the *flâneur*, two further questions need to be confronted, questions of where and when?

First, where? Paris is identified as the paradigm case – Benjamin calls it 'the capital of the nineteenth century' – but can *flânerie* be practised successfully anywhere else? Benjamin occasionally refers to London and Berlin. He doubts the suitability of Rome, partly because its monuments and national shrines are so obtrusive, partly because *flânerie* is supposedly incompatible with the passionate Italian character. Simmel was writing chiefly about his native Berlin, though Paris was also important in shaping his account of city life. Poe's *The Man of the Crowd* was set in London, and many of the notable Parisian *flâneurs* were Anglophiles.

Whether or not *flânerie* is confined to Paris, all commentators see it as a metropolitan rather than provincial phenomenon: Paris, Berlin and London, but not Limoges, Stuttgart or Birmingham. The *flâneur* requires scenes worthy of his regard, and these are to be found in the great imperial capitals. For Shields, *flânerie* involves an imaginative appropriation of empire 'whether on the street, in the arcades and department stores, or in the universal expositions and world fairs' (1994: 75).

Second, when? For Benjamin, the ideal places for *flânerie* were the Parisian arcades (*les passages*). Their golden age was the first half of the nineteenth century. Among the grandest were the revamped Palais Royal (1786), the Passage des Panoramas (1800), the Galerie Vivienne (1823) and the Passage des Princes (1860). Lined with fashionable shops, the arcades featured glass roofs, gas lighting, ironwork, and panelling or paving in marble. Here the art of *flânerie* attained its highest refinement, epitomized for Benjamin in this cameo: 'In 1839 it was considered elegant to take a tortoise out walking. This gives us an idea of the tempo of *flânerie* in the arcades' (Benjamin 1999: 422).

The decline of the arcades set in under the Second Empire with the Haussmannization of Paris. To Benjamin, the Paris of Haussmann's *grands boulevards* was not the heyday of *flânerie* but its silver age. *Flânerie* was threatened by the press of the crowds along the boulevards and by the horse-drawn traffic. This, of course, was the Paris depicted by the impressionists, and it is the Paris identified by many later writers as the *flâneur*'s natural habitat.

These confusions about *flânerie* – doubts about what, where and when – prompt the suspicion that we are discussing not social reality but an urban myth. Why, Shields asks, has there been so much interest in a practice 'which would appear to be marginal, perhaps even elitist, possibly imaginary, and which has been subject to so much mystification?' (1994: 65).

From an anthropological perspective, we can see *flânerie* as a myth – in the sense not of a falsehood but a symbolically charged narrative – which expresses fundamental dynamics and tensions in contemporary urban culture. Viewed in this way, three crucial points stand out.

First, the *flâneur* is not a worker. Benjamin wrote: 'The idleness of the flâneur is a demonstration against the division of labour' (1999: 427). His dandyism signals that he is neither a proletarian nor a bourgeois. His affinity with creative artists dissociates him from respectability and aligns him with bohemia and the *demi-monde*. The *flâneur* is not driven by what Weber called the 'this-worldly asceticism' of the Protestant ethic. He has not been put in this world to carry out God's will, but is an amoral observer pursuing his own autonomous objectives. He evades the moral economy of the class system.

Second, the *flâneur* is not a passive consumer. Talk of the *flâneur*'s window-shopping (Edwards 2000: 22; Bocock 1993: 16) misleadingly suggests that he is in thrall to commodities. Nineteenth-century writing distinguished the true *flâneur* from the mere *badaud*, who gapes greedily and indiscriminately. The *flâneur* is motivated by pure disinterestedness, the quality that Kant defined as essential to the aesthetic gaze (Bourdieu 1984). The *flâneur*'s attention is directed towards obscure and fleeting impressions that escape the casual consumer. Unless he confides his observations to a companion his gaze remains inscrutable. As an example of cultivated *flânerie* (cited by Herbert 1988: 36), consider this account by Antonin Proust of a stroll through Paris with his friend, the painter Edouard Manet:

> I have said what a *flâneur* Manet was. One day we were ascending what has since become the boulevard Malesherbes, in the midst of demolitions intersected by the yawning gaps of already levelled properties. The Monceau district had not yet been laid out. At each step Manet stopped me. Over here a cedar rose up isolated in the midst of a demolished garden. The tree seemed to search under its long arms for the clumps of destroyed flowers. 'You see its skin', he said, 'and the purplish-blue tones of the shadows?' Further along, the wreckers stood out white against the less white walls that were tumbling under their blows, enveloping them in a cloud of dust. Manet remained absorbed for a long time, admiring this spectacle. 'There it is', he cried, 'the symphony in white major of which Théophile Gautier has spoken.'

On the third key issue there is a significant disagreement. The question is, has *flânerie* survived or is it extinct? According to Featherstone, it has found a new arena in the postmodern city. 'The contemporary urban *flâneurs*, or strollers, play with and celebrate the artificiality, randomness and superficiality of the fantastic *mélange* of fictions and strange values which are to be found in the fashions and popular cultures of cities' (Featherstone 1991: 24). Urban life has reached a high point of aestheticization: an intoxicating, hallucinogenic, spectacular world, the fulfilment of surrealism. The postmodern city is less a place of work than a playground. The notion of 'play' is critical: the playful *flâneur* is in control. He bends the world to his will, extracting self-determined pleasure from it. Significantly, contemporary *flânerie* is available to women too. Equally significantly, and fatally, the aspiring *flâneur* is the object of surveillance by close-circuit television cameras. Bauman (1994) may well be right in his verdict on this postmodern *flânerie*: it has been expropriated by consumer capitalism, so that the postmodern *flâneur* is no more than a seduced consumer.

For Benjamin, the *flâneur* is the doomed hero of a degenerate age. His transcendence of the class structure and commodity culture is a short interlude in urban life. Haussmann's projectile boulevards were a decisive blow to *flânerie*. The *grands boulevards* brought with them the *grands magasins,* department stores such as Le Printemps (1865), La Samaritaine (1869), and the opulent Galeries Lafayette (1906). These are places for shoppers, and shoppers are women. As Ferguson says: 'When *flânerie* moves into the private realm of the department store, feminization alters this urban practice almost beyond recognition and jeopardizes, when it does not altogether obliterate, the identification of *flâneur* and artist' (1994: 23).

As well as stimulating commerce, the *grands boulevards* were designed to aid the imperial power's surveillance and control over its populace, hindering the erection of barricades and thereby neutralizing the tactics of urban resistance. The *flâneur* becomes not an observer but the observed. Captured by consumer society, he is a commodity – the ultimate irony. As Benjamin wrote: 'Just as his final ambit is the department store, his last incarnation is the sandwich-man' (1999: 448).

Escape from what and to where?

We have examined three modes of escape from consumer society. Each mode of escape embodies a sociodicy and a soteriology. Sociodicy is the explanation of evil and suffering; a sociodicy will diagnose what is wrong with consumer society. Soteriology is the theory of salvation; a soteriology will tell us what we need to do to be saved.

Cultural omnivorousness is presented as a means of escape from the evil of status distinction. If taste classifies the classifier many of us would be glad to break free from the matrix. If omnivorousness fails, we might follow Finkelstein on the Socratic quest for 'the examined life' (see chapter 1, pp. 20–1). Or we might opt into a religious movement or intentional community that promised an end to status distinction and status striving. Or we might try to give confusing, mixed messages to our audience. Miller et al. (1998: 23) quote a telling passage from Williamson's *Consuming Passions* (1986: 91), in which she writes about the dilemmas of how to dress for the day. How we are perceived, and crucially how we are not perceived, depends on such decisions.

> The black leather skirt rather rules out girlish innocence, oily overalls tend to exclude sophistication, ditto smart suit and radical feminism. Often I have wished I could put them all on together, or appear simultaneously in every possible outfit, just to say, How dare you think any one of these is *me*. But also, See, I can be all of them.

Citizenship is presented as a means of escape from the evil of passivity. Citizens are actively engaged in public life, whereas stupefied consumers wallow or flounder in private enclaves. Obsessed with their needy worries about service delivery, consumers are childishly ignorant of political and economic realities. At the time of writing, the British railway system is in crisis. Consumers complain about filthy rolling stock, harassed staff, trains running late and missed connections. What the consumer wants is a fix: a better service, now. The citizen, in contrast, is aware that these symptoms have complex causes, including underinvestment, ideologically motivated interventions, incessant organizational turmoil, and the attempted destruction of practices through which workers deployed a store of cultural knowledge to make the system work (Strangleman 2003). The citizen might even vote for what the consumer would detest: higher taxes.

Flânerie is presented as an escape from philistinism. The *flâneur* stands aloof from the commodification of culture, seeking salvation in art for art's sake. *Flânerie* is more than a superficial style. Its foundation is educated connoisseurship. If society were dedicated to spreading artistic literacy, *flânerie* would be redundant.

We may, of course, be pessimistic about all these paths to salvation. Cultural omnivorousness may be merely a ploy of sophisticated consumers, citizenship is easily suborned into politically expedient gestures, and *flânerie* quickly degenerates into vain exhibitionism.

Alternatively, we may deny that consumer society is evil. Instead of struggling to escape from it, we might live there happily.

Social exclusion from consumer society

> It is one thing to be poor in a society of producers and universal employment; it is quite a different thing to be poor in a society of consumers, in which life-projects are built around consumer choice rather than work, professional skills, or jobs. If 'being poor' once derived its meaning from the condition of being unemployed, today it draws its meaning primarily from the plight of a flawed consumer. (Bauman 1998: 1)

If it is agreed that society has shifted its basis from production to consumption, then it follows, as Bauman argues, that the nature of poverty and social exclusion will have changed too. Poverty means being prevented from participating in what a society regards as a normal and happy life. In a consumer society, the normal life is the life of the consumer and the happy life is one that delights in consumption. Poor people in a consumer society are those who are socially defined, and self-defined, as defective consumers. Boredom and depression are the psychological consequences. The cure prescribed by consumer society is money, which by definition is what the poor lack.

The traditional collective defence of the poor is no longer available. Time was when poor people could retain their respectability, dignity and pride by observing the rituals of traditional working-class communities, with their prescribed routines for washing clothes, cleaning the house and tending the garden. A scrubbed front doorstep, a neat front room with the pattern on the curtains facing outwards to the street, a garden free from rubbish and weeds, best clothes to wear on Sunday, well-behaved children: these and countless other symbols forged social standing out of adversity. Ritualized propriety was the basis of social order in these communities, reflecting 'the need to create order and meaning in conditions of scarcity and in a context dominated by the nature of factory production' (Martin 1981: 61). This context has disappeared. Neighbourhood communities have no symbolic resources on which they can draw to offset social exclusion from consumer society. The old symbols have lost their meaning, and the only new ones are the symbols of consumer affluence that the poor cannot afford, unless they turn to crime.

Consumer society has sophisticated mechanisms to ensure that the repressed remain excluded. Financial institutions are adept at 'cherry picking' affluent clients who are a good credit risk. Banks are harder to find in poor neighbourhoods, and people who live there discover that their postcode means they will have to pay more for insurance. Financial services are typically offered at a discount if purchased online. Paying by direct debit or standing order from a bank – facilities which the poor may not be able to obtain – is often cheaper than settling by cash or a cheque.

Bauman sees a growing gulf in consumer society between winners and losers. The winners are *the seduced*: consumption, for them, is a vehicle of liberation and self-expression. Their needs have been met by the market, and their life is given over to the acquisition and display of material goods. The losers are *the repressed*, who lack access to the resources needed to participate in consumer life. Their needs have not been met by the market, and they are dependent on inferior support services delivered by cumbersome state bureaucracies.

For much of the time the seduced and the repressed inhabit different worlds. One activity that brings them together is the practice of begging. As Jordan points out, 'begging is ironically an economic activity that is well suited to an age of consumerism, especially when the beggar can confront the consumer at the paradigm moment of their public identity – as a shopper' (1999: 57).

The cities where begging is most active tend to be those which attract affluent tourists, have wide disparities of income between rich and poor, and lack long-standing communities of hardship in which other informal economic activities are available (Jordan 1999: 56). In some cases, such as Edinburgh, begging is a feature of the city's central shopping and tourist areas, while the other varieties of informal and criminal economic activity flourish in the housing estates on the periphery.

Encounters between shoppers and beggars are deeply ambiguous and ambivalent (McIntosh and Erskine 1999). Shoppers typically feel a turmoil of emotions: guilt, embarrassment, sympathy and hostility. People often adopt strategies of avoidance, such as refusing eye-contact, crossing the street and pretending not to hear the requests for money. Some shoppers try to distinguish 'genuine' beggars from impostors, or the deserving poor (such as the homeless) from the undeserving poor (such as drug addicts). Discrimination is not easy, and leads to the irony that people who appear utterly passive and destitute are less likely to evoke sympathy. Shoppers resent having to make such judgements, probably feeling, as Jordan remarks (1999: 55–6), that they have paid their taxes so as not to have to confront a choice between deserving and undeserving cases.

Singled out as a social problem by the former UK Prime Minister, John Major, 'aggressive begging' has the qualities of an urban myth. McIntosh and Erskine's research showed that public criticism of aggression focused on the activities of people raising money for charity, who vigorously rattle tins and buckets 'in people's faces'. The submissive posture of the beggar would not be appropriate for them. They are not destitute people seeking alms, but righteous moral entrepreneurs raising funds for causes whose value they regard as unquestionable.

Beggars, in contrast, usually assume highly demeaning postures. They ask, typically, if the passer-by can 'spare' any 'small change'. Only very tiny sums are involved, yet begging is highly controversial in Western culture. This paradox shows, as McIntosh and Erskine observe (1999: 193), that it is a moral rather than a purely economic transaction.

If beggars, the homeless and other poor people are victims of consumer society, we should beware of blaming the victim. The horizontal axis of figure 1.1 on p. 16 represents the dimension of power, not of rationality.

The poor are regularly accused of behaving irrationally. They waste their money on pointless and even harmful pursuits: alcohol, tobacco and gambling. They are not capable of deferring gratification, so if they have a windfall gain they immediately spend it in a self-indulgent binge. The women are little better than the men. The improvident housewife wastes money on junk food instead of preparing wholesome meals from nutritious ingredients. The culture of poverty locks people into behaviours that make it impossible for them to escape from poverty. If only they would do what their middle-class advisers tell them, they might become rational actors.

Research on the coping strategies of the poor (usefully summarized in Walker and Collins, forthcoming) has demonstrated that, contrary to the stereotype of feckless improvidence, they employ a high level of personal, economic and social skills to cope with the constraints of poverty. It is, typically, women's work. They plan budgets meticulously to the last penny. They set aside money for later, sometimes hiding it from other family members. They make shopping lists and stick to them. They keep a running total of expenditure as they progress round the supermarket. They are sensitive to price variations, and scour the shops for genuine bargains. They shop frequently not through self-indulgence, but to avoid building up a store of purchases that children and menfolk could raid. Cigarettes are knowingly used to suppress appetite, to reduce stress, and as a reward and solace. They buy so-called junk food because they know it will not be wasted, and give food to children on demand for the same reason. They prioritize feeding, clothing and educating their children over their own needs. They engage actively in bartering systems as a means of increasing household resources.

A particular problem for poor people is the pressure from children to purchase goods that carry status. Children are adept at exploiting the situation, playing on the guilt and embarrassment that parents feel, and exploiting any inconsistencies in their approach. Purchasing and displaying branded goods, particularly clothes, are an important marker of status for young people, and play a part in strengthening their self-confidence (Miles 2000: 135–7). Poor people striving to consume rationally have to accommodate the demands of children for whom consumption is the key to communication.

Consumption and new forms of community

Within Western discourse on consumption there is a recurrent opposition between community and consumerism as ways of life. They are presented as incompatible, but are they?

Social change has undoubtedly eroded much of the infrastructure on which traditional communities depended. The decline of manufacturing has decimated industries such as iron and steel, the docks, coal mining, and the communities they supported. The ritualism that characterized such communities has given way to more privatized, home and nuclear-family centred styles of life and companionate ideals of marriage. In the countryside, mechanization of agriculture, rural depopulation, withdrawal of public and private services, and an influx of commuters and second-home buyers have combined to shatter countless rural idylls.

Local social systems are increasingly penetrated by national and global forces. The growth of car ownership and geographical mobility, the development of efficient telecommunications, the rationalization of retailing, global tourism, the omnipresence of television: these all reduce reliance on local provision of employment, entertainment, goods, services, and information. For Meyrowitz, the electronic media have detached social situations from their physical setting, obliterating loyalty to territory, so that we have become 'hunters and gatherers of an information age', citizens of an 'essentially placeless' culture (1985: 316–17). Pursuing this notion, Giddens argues that place has become 'phantasmagoric' (1990; 1991): as knowledgeable social actors, we are uneasily aware that the global has engulfed the local.

An unblinking examination of the social conditions that gave rise to traditional communities reveals, in Williams's graphic phrase, 'the mutuality of the oppressed' (1973: 104). Thus, in their classic study of St Ann's in Nottingham, Coates and Silburn (1970) document the joyless burden of intractable practical problems and lack of privacy imposed by poor housing: the cramped conditions, the damp, the thin partitions, the shared lavatories. Even among sociologists, it is seldom recognized that back-to-back housing was exactly that: houses sharing not two but *three* party walls. In traditional working-class communities, as is well known, the home is not a place to entertain friends. This is not an arbitrary free-floating norm of traditional working-class culture, but a rational self-protective response to material constraints. When St Ann's was redeveloped, former residents typically welcomed the enhanced quality of social life made possible by modern housing.

Sentimentality about community is a product of the soft-focus lens. Social scientists have learned to ask hard questions: who does what, for whom, why, for how long, with what resources and with what consequences? The convivial round of drinks in the local pub, the free advice over the garden fence, the borrowed bag of sugar: how do these happy images of the local community connect with, say, the problem of caring for a frail incontinent person suffering memory loss and violent mood swings brought about by Alzheimer's syndrome? The verdict of the literature is clear: sociability is not to be confused with service delivery, the burdens of caring can be physically and emotionally devastating, and at the sharp end we find not friends and neighbours but kin. Among kin, while the role of men should not be overlooked, the principal responsibility and the most taxing cases 'naturally' fall to women, specifically to daughters.

Lewis and Meredith's (1988) study of women who lived with and cared for their mothers showed the dark side of family duty. It involves feelings of guilt, resentment and frustration, fear of failure, exhaustion, severing of social ties, strained relations with other kin, taboos on talking about illness and dying, coping with personality changes in the mother, adjusting to the mother's institutionalization or death, and the carer's anxiety about her own health and ageing.

Co-resident caring for mothers by daughters is likely to decline. The women in Lewis and Meredith's study were mostly in their forties and fifties, and 70 per cent of them were single. They had grown up in the 1940s and 1950s, in an era when traditional gender roles were more likely to be internalized, when women were less attached to labour market and career, and when the norm was that a daughter would live with her parents until her own marriage. Many daughters had drifted into the caring role, partly to cope with the stigma of spinsterhood and childlessness. Even among these women, reciprocity was vital to the achievement of a satisfying caring relationship, involving 'the give and take characteristic of deep companionship and mutual interdependence' (Lewis and Meredith 1988: 51).

What does not follow from this is that kinship is a fixed set of rights and duties monitored and enforced by a social entity known as 'the kinship system'. Finch and Mason's research in Greater Manchester shows that the kin group is typically seen as 'a safety-net which should be used as a last resort, not a first resort' (1993: 164). A good deal of effort is devoted to *avoiding* asking kin for help. Kin responsibilities are not prescribed duties, still less rights; they are fluid 'guidelines' that are predominantly procedural rather than substantive. Kin responsibilities are calculated and negotiated; they are not fixed at birth but develop or atrophy over time, depending on a complex system of reciprocity in which not just material resources but personal reputations and identities are at stake. Parents' or guardians' responsibility for their children is the main personal relationship where socially, and in law, our society imposes duties. Relatives should not even expect assistance, let alone demand it. Finch and Mason point out (1993: 180) that attempts by government to redraw the boundaries between the state and family, and to extend the range of family responsibilities, run counter to contemporary realities.

The rhetoric of community remains as powerful as ever, as does the yearning for fulfilment in 'communion' with others. The pull of community is felt on the left as well as the right, and by social reformers as well as social reactionaries. For some, the paradigm community was the Greek city state, the *polis*. Industrialization, urbanization and the progressive division of labour were seen to produce a conflict-ridden dehumanized society peopled not by the 'whole men' of Athens but by segmented role-players.

The spirit of our age is democratic, anti-authoritarian and egalitarian. It is in tension with the family, which is essentially hierarchical. The kinship system is adapting to contemporary culture by becoming more flexible. Within families, liking and dislike has become ever more important:

kinship ties are optional, and marriages are more akin to friendship. Parents' responsibility for their children is the only kinship tie that is mandatory.

Social order is no longer based on kinship obligations, or civic responsibility, or the norms and values of deprived and socially isolated communities. Nor does individualized consumption in a mass society provide a foundation for social cohesion. Governments across the First World are attracted by the claims made for communitarianism to fill the void, and look for ways to boost the level of social capital among the poor and disadvantaged. The search is on for a socially engineered 'Third Way' between the rigours of free market capitalism and the discredited vision of the command economy and planned society.

In a highly original approach to these problems, Ray Pahl (2000) has emphasized the significance of a social formation that has been curiously neglected: friendship. In social scientific thinking, friendship has typically been seen as a very pale relation of kinship, on the 'blood is thicker than water' principle. If there was a golden age of friendship it lies in the irretrievable past: in ancient Greece and Rome, or the early Christian church. As with so much else, the story is told as one of decline from past glory. Georg Simmel argued at the beginning of the twentieth century that the citizens of the modern metropolis are forced to adopt a mistrustful, blasé attitude as a necessary means of survival (Simmel 1971/1903). The division of labour parcels up our lives into specialized roles, preventing us from relating to one another as whole human beings. The bleak competitive struggle requires us to behave as rational self-seeking actors. The world of work has been transformed, so that exchanges of job security for company loyalty are now rare, even in Japan. Work is a low-trust environment, in which it is vital to keep exit lines open. One consequence is that we are less likely to find trusted friends at work. We must take care not to reveal ourselves to colleagues in case we betray something that might be used against us. We have to show no weakness and tough it out. In the modern workplace, colleagues are no more than passing acquaintances. It is an age of suspicion. This milieu is judged to be utterly unfavourable to the cultivation of friendship as traditionally understood.

Perhaps, though, this analysis is too pessimistic, and friendship can flourish precisely because trust is absent elsewhere. If we live in a risk society beset by doubt, anxiety and malaise, one way to deal with the stress is, as Pahl says, 'to form good relationships' (2000: 172). Friendship is well suited to a consumer society, not least because it is rooted in choice and can survive the collapse of community as conventionally understood. It is tempting to refer to friendship as a social network, but as Pahl points out this is misleading. My friends' friends typically mean little or nothing to me, because I did not choose them. Friendship is, rather, a 'personal community', a 'social convoy' of friends whose membership fluctuates as we move through life.

Far from being hostile to friendship, modern life has features that help to foster it. The expansion of higher education has increased our capacity for making friends; the impact on women is particularly significant. Student years are a time for forging a common past: coping with examinations, exploring relationships, sharing a house. Although not a substitute for face-to-face contact, telecommunications enable us to keep in touch with friends despite the fact that we are geographically mobile and time-pressured. Consumer society may be the golden age of friendship.

5
McDonaldization and Disneyization

McDonaldization: life in the iron cage

'The process by which the principles of the fast-food restaurant are coming to dominate more and more sectors of American society as well as of the rest of the world' (Ritzer 1996: 1): George Ritzer's concept of McDonaldization, succinctly expressed in that one sentence, has provoked an occasionally acrimonious debate about the past, present and future of consumer society.

Ritzer has repeatedly emphasized that his concept of McDonaldization is built on the foundation of Max Weber's work on rationalization. For Weber, modernity brings a decline in the authority both of tradition and of charismatic leaders. In their place stands legal-rational authority: legal in that it is based on codified rules, rational in that the rules are justified on the grounds of their fairness, equity and effectiveness. The structural form in which legal-rational authority is embedded is bureaucracy.

Rationalization carries with it what Weber called *die Entzauberung der Welt*. Normally translated as the disenchantment of the world, Weber's phrase means literally the removal of magic from the world. It refers to a profound process by which Western society and culture have been transformed – in the arts, science, medicine, the law, politics and the economy.

Claiming a pedigree from Weber, Ritzer's account of McDonaldization identifies four components.

Efficiency In a time-pressured society, McDonaldized services are desired because they are *fast*.

Calculability McDonaldized services are quantified: the customer's burger and fries are an exact size, and are delivered within a specified time. Quality is redefined as quantity: McDonaldized products, as famously with the Mac burger, claim to be *big*.

Predictability The social anthropologist Lévi-Strauss said of mythology that it was a machinery for the suppression of time. McDonaldization, I would argue, has a greater claim: it is a machinery for the suppression of time and place. McDonaldized products and services are standardized at all times and everywhere. They are *the same*.

Control Wherever possible, technology is substituted for human labour. McDonaldized goods and services are *automated*.

As Ritzer's definition implies, McDonaldization is not confined to the fast-food industry, let alone to one company operating in it. McDonald's is a paradigm case, but there are many others. Ritzer says that he might have called the process Burger Kingization, Seven Elevenization, Fuddruckerization, H&R Blockization, Kinder Care-ization, Jiffy Lube-ization, or Nutri/Systemization – but McDonaldization sounded better.

McDonaldization is not just about products. Its principles embrace workers, managers and consumers in a mesh of McDonaldized relationships. Workers have McJobs – routine, unskilled, machine-paced – as do all but the most senior managers. As for customers, their brief interactions with McService providers are carefully scripted with pseudo-convivial wishes of 'a nice day' and mock-concerned requests to contemplate having fries 'with that'. The customer has become a compliant McConsumer.

A key theme of Ritzer's critique of McDonaldization is his challenge to its claim to efficiency, calculability, predictability and control. In the style of the Frankfurt School his is an 'immanent critique', exposing what he calls 'the irrationality of rationality' – which he sees as the fifth, hidden dimension of McDonaldization.

Although Ritzer himself does not explicitly make the distinctions in this way, I suggest that three aspects of his irrationality of rationality can be distinguished: illusion, externalities and dehumanization.

Illusion

Two aspects of McDonaldization are real enough. First, they are predictable. This is one of their outstanding advantages: wherever you are, you know what to expect. McDonalds itself has to make some concessions to indigenous cultures – burgers made of beef do not sell to Hindus – but these are kept to the minimum necessary. A risk-averse traveller in a foreign land who does not speak the language and knows little of the culture can rely on McDonalds. It may not offer the most refined meal available, and the ambience is scarcely rich in local colour, but at least the food is prepared hygienically, so the tourist's holiday is unlikely to be ruined by gastric disorders. The staff will not insult you, and your nationality, 'race' or religion will not count against you. It is a safe environment for all, including women and children, free from drunken behaviour and undesired soliciting. Similarly, the tourist who rents a car from Hertz or Avis knows that she will get a low-mileage, well-maintained vehicle. A local hire firm may offer a better deal, or may not. In the absence of local knowledge, and assuming she is not on a shoe-string budget, it is entirely rational for a risk-averse tourist to opt for one of the major service providers.

Nor is there any obvious illusion about a McDonaldized company's control over customers and employees. Ritzer's account is indisputably accurate: 'The people who eat in fast-food restaurants are controlled, albeit (usually) subtly. Lines, limited menus, few options, and uncomfortable seats all lead diners to do what management wishes them to do – eat quickly and leave early. Further, the drive-through (in some cases walk-through) window leads diners to leave before they eat' (1996: 11). What is true of customers holds for employees: the work is unskilled, rigidly and minutely prescribed, fully scripted, closely monitored and increasingly automated. It affords little scope for the exercise of skill, discretion and the personal touch. Depart from the job specification or the script, and they fire you.

If the predictability and control achieved by McDonaldized services is real enough, their apparent efficiency *is* an illusion, Ritzer claims. They are indeed fast, but this speed is achieved by getting the customer to do a lot of the work: to stand in a queue, pay immediately, carry his food to the table, and dispose of the remains afterwards. It is not just the staff but the consumers who have to move quickly. Self-service may be efficient – but for whom?

Because they need to monitor their staff closely, McDonaldized companies typically suffer from low morale, low productivity and high labour turnover. The only obvious solution is automation, substituting capital for labour. This may succeed, but it cannot deal with a deeper inefficiency: failure to innovate. The same old goods and services are endlessly reproduced. It may be a winning formula, but only until times change. When they do, McDonaldized companies are poorly placed to respond. They may redesign the packaging and seek to reposition themselves symbolically, but basically they do what they do, take it or leave it. If people decide to leave it, McDonaldized companies are stuck.

The calculability of McDonaldized companies also involves an illusion. Quality is redefined as quantity: Big Macs, Whoppers, Biggies. Not only is collapsing quality into quantity a deception, so too are the quantities themselves. Nutritional analysis indicates that some of these products are less than they claim. If anything is big it is the profit margins.

Higher education, on Ritzer's account (1996: 64–8), has not been immune to McDonaldization. Quantitative measures of staff and student productivity abound. In the USA, the grade-point average is a cultural fetish. Teachers writing references for students are asked to rank them in comparison with their peers (upper 5 per cent and so on). Credentialism, the proliferation of paper qualifications, is rampant. Academics must publish in bulk, or perish. Citation indices are taken as the indicator of quality. In the UK, a regular Research Assessment Exercise rates the performance of all academic departments on a scale rising from 1 to 5*; the outcome is fateful for a department's funding and individual careers. Teaching Quality has also been assessed, on a scale of 6 to 24. In the case of these rationalized regulatory exercises, irrationalities are apparent, not least the regulatory burdens which, in true McDonaldized fashion, remain totally uncosted. This brings us to the second major aspect of Ritzer's analysis of the irrationality of rationality.

Externalities

McDonaldized companies are skilled at passing costs on to others who are forced to bear them. Putting customers to work is one example. Ritzer also emphasizes the environmental impact of McDonaldization, with its profligate use of resources and creation of non-biodegradable waste products. Companies make a show of environmental concern, for example setting their employees to remove rubbish from the pavements, or launching educational programmes to raise ecological consciousness. Show is all this is: promotional gesture, not a serious attempt to bear the full costs of production. The corporations' more powerful weapon is to threaten legal action against critics. Corporations with a lovable image are apt to turn nasty if we refuse to love them.

Dehumanization

This is the heart of Ritzer's critique of McDonaldization. McDonaldized corporations dehumanize their employees, who resent the close monitoring of their work and the flagrant attempts to extinguish skill and discretion. Their response is the familiar pattern of low morale, absenteeism and high labour turnover, which sets in train an endless spiral of tighter controls followed by greater resentment followed by tighter controls.

What is true of employees is true of customers. Despite all the illusions of the fast-food industry – the friendliness, the fun, the myths of choice and value for money – the dining experience is dehumanized and functional: 'The best that can usually be said is that it is efficient and it is over quickly' (Ritzer 1996: 131). Here Ritzer forgets that even the efficiency is a mirage.

Dehumanized workers, dehumanized customers: how could social interaction between them be anything other than dehumanized? Workers and customers are forced into inauthentic, scripted pseudo-relationships while remaining total strangers. High labour turnover means that staff do not typically form personal relationships among themselves: not much camaraderie among the crew. Even the customers are discouraged from interacting with one another, and are made to dine at separate bolted-down tables. McDonaldization has spread from the restaurant to the home, facilitated by the microwave oven, which empowers even the most incompetent adolescent to heat up a meal for himself any time he likes.

Three factors are identified as driving McDonaldization forward (Ritzer 1996: 144–8). First, profitability. Cheap labour, economies of scale, rapid throughput, tight managerial control – in short, a capitalist's paradise. Second, Ritzer points to a distinctively American, sentimental celebration of McDonaldization. Since these corporations are selling not just products but a lifestyle, their brands often become patriotic symbols of national identity. The trick is to turn this into a marketing advantage not just at home but internationally, as in the song: 'I'd like to buy the world a Coke . . .' American patriotism and cultural imperialism are made to harmonize. Third, McDonaldization is attuned to wider trends in society. More women have paid employment; there are more dual career and lone parent families; people travel long distances, often by car; affluence means people are prepared to spend money to save time and labour; mass media advertising has facilitated the spread of brands; and developments in food and other technologies have made it all possible.

Given all the factors driving McDonaldization, is its triumph inevitable? Ritzer discusses various means of resistance (1996: 198–204), but they appear to be the desperate measures of defeated guerrillas. We can lobby to make our views felt – but McDonaldized institutions respond only when the pressure becomes overwhelming, which is seldom. They are, in any case, limited in what they can do by the very nature of McDonaldization, which is a straitjacket for them as well as for us. If we cannot easily exercise voice, what about exit? We may patronize non-McDonaldized organizations, if we can find any. One problem we face is that many McDonaldized organizations seek to pass themselves off as something else. Even when they try to preserve the principles on which they were founded, commercial success and organizational growth make it harder for firms to resist rationalization. Ritzer discusses the case of Ben & Jerry's 'caring capitalism' (Ritzer 1996: 191–5). In the early days, when Ben Cohen and Jerry Greenfield began selling ice cream in a refurbished petrol station in 1978, they were charismatic visionaries with a mission to produce a high quality product rather than to maximize profits. They deliberately sought to avoid rationalization and the corporate embrace, but found this more and more difficult as the company expanded and eventually become international in scope.

The tendency of McDonaldization to colonize alternatives to it is examined by Tester (1999) in his discussion of vegetarianism. He distinguishes between *ethical vegetarianism*, which implies that people are morally concerned with the treatment of animals, and *lifestyle vegetarianism*, which reflects people's preoccupations with nutrition and the risks of consuming meat. Lifestyle vegetarianism can readily be McDonaldized but ethical vegetarianism cannot, because it is an absolute, categorical moral commitment.

Tester's analysis does not refute the McDonaldization thesis but confirms it. Ethical vegetarianism is, in Weber's terms, substantively rational, embodying a commitment to ethical principles. On a Weberian perspective, substantive rationality is swamped by formal instrumental rationality. Individuals may opt out into dissident subcultures – charismatically led religious movements, for example – but their position is marginal to the trajectory of social change and has minimal impact on it. Individual opt-outs do not add up to significant cultural resistance. As Tester himself comments, lifestyle vegetarianism is the culturally dominant form of vegetarianism, and it is open to commercial exploitation by McDonaldized corporations – a process I am tempted to call Veggieburgerization.

Higher education is a recurrent example in Ritzer's discussion of the McDonaldization thesis. He discusses the tyranny of the timetable, the widespread use of computer-graded multiple-choice examinations, and the dehumanizing impact of large class sizes. In his list of actions that people can take to combat or evade the McDonaldization of universities, he gives this advice to students: 'Avoid classes with short-answer tests graded by computer. If a computer-graded exam is unavoidable, make extraneous marks and curl the edges of the exam so that the computer cannot deal with it. Seek out small classes; get to know your professors' (Ritzer 1996: 201).

Ritzer admits that some of his advice is offered tongue-in-cheek. The above is presumably an example. No student would make the mistake of deliberately defacing a computer-read examination script: all this would produce is a mark of zero. Classes may be small because the course is poor and the teacher incompetent. Even more likely, there will be no small classes. Teachers may themselves prefer greater human contact with students, but be so time-pressured that they cannot afford the luxury. If the whole of the higher education system is becoming relentlessly McDonaldized, the tactics of resistance proposed by Ritzer are not practical politics but a romantic fantasy.

Ritzer's suggested tactics are also strikingly individualistic. He appears to see little scope for collective action. In his metaphor of society as an iron, velvet or rubber cage (see pp. 124–5 below), he does not allow for the possibility of an organized mass break-out.

Undoubtedly the most stinging criticism of *The McDonaldization of Society* is O'Neill's charge that it is a McText, as bland as any fast-food hamburger (O'Neill 1999). Ritzer responded to this attack, which he found offensive, by pointing out that he had denounced unchallenging textbooks that spoon-feed students with pap. But has he written one himself? Is his McDonaldization a palatable but simplified version of Weber's scholarly, subtle and profound work on rationalization? In his own defence, Ritzer (1999a) underlines the moral outrage in his book, its critique of McDonaldized education, and its Weberian analysis of dehumanization as the supreme irrationality of rationality.

Disneyization: entering the Magic Kingdom

'The process by which *the principles* of the Disney theme parks are coming to dominate more and more sectors of American society as well as the rest of the world' (Bryman 1999a: 26). Alan Bryman's concept of Disneyization is deliberately formulated to invite comparison and contrast with McDonaldization. He emphasizes that the process is not about the rise of the Disney corporation and its multiple enterprises, but about the principles on which they rest. McDonaldization and Disneyization refer to far more than the commercial success of two corporations.

Bryman's work on Disneyization is an analysis of a trend, not a critique of a culture. He rejects the rival term 'Disneyfication' precisely because it is deliberately pejorative (Bryman 1999a: 26–7). Disneyfication implies distortion, stereotyping, sanitization, escapism, sentimentality and banality. Sometimes it implies an insidious form of cultural imperialism, expressed most strongly by French protestors who labelled Euro Disneyland a 'cultural Chernobyl'.

In parallel to Ritzer, Bryman identifies four key elements in Disneyization.

Theming Theming occurs when artefacts, characters and narratives not directly related to an activity are imported into it in order to embellish it with symbolism. Theming is widespread in the service sector, with restaurants, pubs, bars, hotels, casinos, shopping malls and amusement parks all being heavily themed. From Julius Caesar and Ancient Rome to Henry VIII and Merrie England, and from Davy Crockett and the Wild West to Captain James T. Kirk and the Final

Frontier, theming presents itself as a cultural phenomenon to be sought after (or avoided).

Dedifferentiation of consumption Dedifferentiation involves the erosion of conventional boundaries between institutional orders, thereby blurring formerly distinct concepts and categories. It means that 'forms of consumption associated with different institutional spheres become interlocked with each other and increasingly difficult to distinguish' (Bryman 1999a: 33). Thus the Disney theme parks bring together and intermingle shops, restaurants, hotels, merchandise, and rides. Entertainment and education are merged (arguably one reason why the Disney parks are unpopular with intellectuals, for whom education must be pure and untainted by titillation of popular taste). The objective is to create an encompassing Disney experience in which different forms of consumption blend into one another. Staying at one of the Disney hotels, which are located within the parks' perimeters and are themselves themed, is part of the total package rather than an adjunct to it. There are also practical advantages. Consumers who choose to stay at a Disney hotel are able to enter the parks early before the mass of tourists arrive, and have priority booking of tables in the most popular restaurants.

Merchandizing The Disney theme parks offer countless opportunities to purchase goods bearing copyright images and logos. Merchandise is a major source of profit for the corporation. This has been true from the early days. Walt Disney was a perfectionist who demanded the highest technical quality in his animations. This cut into his profits, so he used the revenues from Disney merchandise to subsidize the motion pictures. As Bryman explains (1995: 6–7; 1999a: 36), Disney learned the significance of copyright images early in his career. His first commercial success was a cartoon series featuring Oswald the Lucky Rabbit. Oswald generated a range of profitable merchandise, for which Disney received nothing. When he tried to negotiate a new contract, he found that the distributor, Universal Pictures, had retained the right to use the Oswald name and character. Disney never repeated his mistake. Abandoning Oswald, he began work on a character he planned to call Mortimer. His wife Lillian persuaded him that a better name would be Mickey.

Emotional labour   Employees in the Disney theme parks are required to display appropriate emotions during service encounters (Hochschild 1983; see chapter 2, pp. 49–50 above). Not only must they be friendly and helpful, they must also be seen to be sharing in the fun; this is not work but play. As Hochschild observed, what the corporation wants is *deep* acting. Employees are meant to feel the emotions they exhibit, which means that corporate culture has to be internalized. To make this possible, Disney has developed a special vocabulary that all its employees are expected to use (Bryman 1995: 108). Customers are *guests*, employees are *hosts, hostesses* or *cast members*, hiring is *casting*, interviews are *auditions*, uniforms are *costumes*, designers are *imagineers*, talking robots are *audio-animatronic figures*, and queues are *pre-entertainment areas*. It is a unique mix of family imagery, euphemism, and the language of show business.

McDonaldization and Disneyization compared

Neither Bryman nor Ritzer is claiming that McDonaldization and Disneyization are mutually exclusive, competing trends. Both authors argue that there is a high degree of overlap between them.

McDonaldized companies can incorporate elements of Disneyization. Bryman points out that many McDonaldized companies draw on two elements of Disneyization: theming and emotional labour. In contrast, they place less emphasis on merchandise other than their primary products and services. As highly rationalized organizations they also tend not to be sites of the dedifferentiation of consumption. They offer specialized goods and services, and aim to be fast: concentration, not distraction, is the rationale of their business.

Conversely, Disneyized companies are typically McDonaldized. This is true of Disney itself. According to Bryman, three of Ritzer's four dimensions are characteristic of the Disney corporation. Disney is profitable and *efficient*. Its theme parks offer a *predictable*, safe environment free from unpleasant surprises. It exercises subtle *control* over visitors and tight discipline over employees. For several years after the opening of Euro Disneyland, male cast members were required to be clean-shaven, even if their facial hair was hidden beneath their Donald Duck costume, and despite the fact that Walt Disney himself sported a moustache.

Unlike Bryman, Ritzer is inclined to interpret Disneyization not as a significant cultural innovation but simply as a variant of McDonaldization. The Disney theme parks are what he calls 'cathedrals of consumption', and are extremely efficient at shifting merchandise. They are enchanted – but the enchantment is simulated, self-referential and temporary. It is a feeble shadow of Weber's notion of an enchanted world in which the here-and-now is suffused with what Berger (1970) calls 'signals of transcendence'. Whereas medieval cathedrals are full of rich symbols that point to an ultimate reality that imparts meaning to human existence, modern cathedrals of consumption merely invite a question they cannot answer: 'how to live a more meaningful life within a society increasingly defined by consumption?' (Ritzer 1999b: 217).

Quantity versus quality

Ritzer's fourth dimension of McDonaldization, *calculability*, is on Bryman's assessment not so clearly applicable to the Disney parks. It is one of the major ways in which Bryman's analysis differs from Ritzer's, differences that are summarized in the box.

McDonaldization	Disneyization
Quantity	Quality
Dupes and victims	Communicators and rational actors
Illusion of choice	Reality of choice

Ritzer argues that McDonaldized corporations redefine quality as quantity. Size may often be an illusion, but it is the distorted measure by which quality is gauged. For Ritzer, McDonaldized companies rarely offer products and services of genuinely high quality. An exception, he believes, is Starbucks (Ritzer 1996: 153). Their coffee is expensive, but it is a high quality product. His explanation is that Starbucks has a simple product, coffee beans, which they brew using modern technology that guarantees a good result. His hypothesis is that simple products can be McDonaldized without sacrificing quality, but complex products cannot be.

It may well be that Ritzer overstates his case. Many organizations refer to quantitative measures as a badge of quality, such as volume of sales, throughput of customers, or a five-star rating for research. The omnipresence of quantification is a revealing trait of Western societies – a feature reinforced by value-for-money consumerism, which demands objective quantified data. It does not necessarily follow that quality has been sacrificed.

As for the Disney theme parks, Bryman argues that they are 'islands of quality' (1995: 126). Walt Disney was determined that his facilities should have none of the tawdriness of amusement parks like Coney Island, whose 'carney' atmosphere played to working-class ideals of an exuberant day out (Bryman 1995: 93). The Disney parks are clean, tidy and regulated, the hotels well-equipped and fully staffed, and the rides engineered and maintained to the most demanding standards of safety. They are environments in which visitors have every reason to feel safe and comfortable. They are not to everybody's taste – what is? – but that is not a valid ground for questioning their quality.

Dupes and victims versus communicators and rational actors

The customer who patronizes McDonaldized outlets is, on Ritzer's account, at least in part a victim or dupe. These companies trade on illusions of quality-as-quantity, pass costs on to customers and the wider society, dehumanize staff and consumers, and reduce social interaction to the insincere recital of anodyne scripts. If this is their impact, Ritzer is justified in recommending tactics of evasion and resistance.

Are the staff themselves victims and dupes? For all the demands Disney places on its employees, labour turnover is low. The corporation ties its staff with golden chains, such as subsidized meals, and promotes a high proportion of its senior staff through the ranks. In contrast to McDonaldized companies, it does not offer McJobs. Perhaps, as Bryman hints, the emotional labour has a degree of authenticity, and Disney cast members do gain some satisfaction from entertaining the customers?

Turning to theming, Ritzer implies that only dupes and victims would patronize establishments that are heavily themed. He argues that such restaurants have to rely on elaborate theming to offset the lacklustre quality of the food (Ritzer 1999b: 119). Beardsworth and Bryman's analysis of themed restaurants suggests, in contrast, that consumers are neither dupes nor victims. Theming involves what they call *quasification*, from the Latin word *quasi*, meaning 'as if'. Quasification is 'a general process of fabricating an environment which can be experienced *as if it were something other* than the mere mechanics of its mundane production' (Beardsworth and Bryman 1999: 249). Following Beck (1992), they develop the idea that modern life is experienced as bringing chronic low-level risk, which generates anxiety without excitement or stimulation. Quasification makes possible 'temporary escape from the direct contemplation of the irony of the relationship between tedium and security' (Beardsworth and Bryman 1999: 250); it lifts us out of everyday routine.

To work, quasification has to be a collaboration between those who engineer and those who consume it. Beardsworth and Bryman draw a parallel with Roland Barthes's famous essay on wrestling (Barthes 1972/1957: 15–25). The contrived nature of wrestling is the point; it is not sport but a form of pantomime, and its consumers are sophisticates. They have not been duped into thinking it is a sporting contest between two athletes struggling to win. Nor are they victims of a crude swindle to extract money for a sham. Spectators do not need a cultural critic to inform them that the wrestlers are acting their parts (fair sportsman versus evil cheat, plucky underdog versus undisputed champion) and that the contest is rigged. Unlike some other cultural forms, wrestling is healthy precisely because everyone knows it is an artifice.

So too with themed restaurants. The themes are drawn from popular culture and easily recognized. A high level of cultural capital in Bourdieu's sense is not required to interpret them, but what consumers do possess is *virtual capital*: 'a fluent familiarity with the techniques and forms used to create representations of exotic settings, distant time periods, unfamiliar cultures and remote events' (Beardsworth and Bryman 1999: 252). The designers of themed environments rely on consumers possessing a high level of virtual capital so that they can enjoy the joke. The success of the enterprise is predicated upon the knowing participation of consumers who are communicators acting rationally.

The illusion of choice versus the reality of choice

Towards the end of *The McDonaldization of Society*, Ritzer distinguishes three perspectives on the Weber-inspired thesis that McDonaldization, like bureaucratic rationality, is an iron cage.

First, some people believe that the bars of the cage are made of velvet. They appreciate security, predictability and impersonality. These people, whom Ritzer fears are a growing proportion of the populations of First World societies, are so familiar with McDonaldization that they may not be able even to conceive of alternatives.

Second, for some people the bars are made of rubber, and can be stretched sufficiently to allow for an escape from time to time. McDonaldized companies have their uses – notably, their speedy service may help us to get on with the rest of our lives – but at other times we prefer non-McDonaldized alternatives. Ritzer adds that 'while the bars may seem like rubber, they are still there' (1996: 178).

Third, following Weber, some people believe the bars are made of iron. They see that escapes can be no more than brief moments of respite snatched before McDonaldization closes in again. 'They share', Ritzer says, 'the dark and pessimistic outlook of Weber and me . . .' (1996: 178).

Despairing of people who like living in a cage with velvet bars, Ritzer offers advice to everyone else about how to escape, if only for a brief interlude. The overwhelming impression he conveys is that McDonaldization is ultimately irresistible. *This is shown by a curious feature of his own metaphor.* The point about the velvet cage is that people are comfortable in it, and either see no reason to escape or do not even accept that they are in a cage. The composition of the bars, velvet or otherwise, is therefore irrelevant. They can be made of iron, but the inhabitants will still be contented.

What of the rubber cage? Ritzer suggests that its inmates are sometimes happy and sometimes not. They can escape for a while, because the bars can be stretched – but then what? Is Ritzer's point that these people let themselves back into the cage when they have taken a stroll outside? Or are they captured and put back in? Or do they simply find themselves in another cage, so that there is an infinite series of cages within cages? How, then, does a rubber cage differ from an iron cage? Is it simply that it is even harder to escape if the bars are made of iron? And what will happen if we do escape? Or is the point that escape is impossible?

The latter seems to be Ritzer's implication. His book ends by quoting Dylan Thomas's poem, *Do not go gentle into that good night.* The message is that not two but three things are unavoidable: death, taxes – and McDonaldization.

How, according to Bryman, can we resist the form of McDonaldized tourism that manifests itself in visits to Disney theme parks? The immediate answer is clear: *don't go* (Bryman 1999b: 112). At one level, this answer is obviously not meant to be taken seriously. If McDonaldization is colonizing all tourist experiences, 'not going' is not an option. The question is, how deep does McDonaldization run? For Ritzer, a sociologist who wears the mantle of Weberian cultural pessimism, we are fighting against an overwhelming tide that will probably engulf us all. As his very definition of the term implies, McDonaldization is a form of cultural imperialism that is spreading out from the USA to encompass the globe. Bryman, in contrast, is far less pessimistic about

Disneyization: we really do have the option not to take part in it. Perhaps Disneyization is simply less invasive than McDonaldization. Alternatively, perhaps cultural pessimists like Ritzer underestimate people's capacity to resist, and to do so collectively.

Tellingly, Bryman received no cooperation whatsoever from the Disney Corporation, which is suspicious of anything it cannot control. The darker side of Disneyization is certainly addressed in his work, particularly the omnipresent surveillance and discipline. Even so, it may be that Bryman's principal sites of Disneyization – theme parks and themed restaurants – are relatively benign. Why worry about other people's choice of holiday destination or place to eat? When Disneyized experiences are a temporary respite from the stress of contemporary life, all may be well. But what if a taste for the artificial obliterates the desire for anything else? Disney has built not just theme parks for tourists but a town, Celebration, in which people live and work. Like Disney World five miles to the north, Celebration is a clean, orderly and policed environment – a self-conscious blueprint of the good community. It is equipped with all the amenities a properly socialized resident could wish; there is no need to leave. Disneyization may be benign if it is a part of life, but what if it is the whole?

The box above omits one distinction that might be drawn between McDonaldization and Disneyization: the contrast between modernity and postmodernity. On the one hand, Ritzer's analysis of the dimensions of McDonaldization identifies efficiency, calculability, predictability and control – all classic features of modernist rationality. Disneyization, on the other hand, involves postmodern elements of play, self-indulgence and fantasy. Disney is, after all, the Magic Kingdom.

One problem with this fourth contrast is that Disneyized companies are organized on rational modernist lines rather than on postmodern principles. This is true of the Disney corporation itself. In Weberian terms it is a rational bureaucracy, hierarchically structured and controlled by a central authority whose pursuit of predictability necessarily quashes individual non-conformist departures from corporate guidelines. In Ritzer's terms, it is McDonaldized. The one respect, ironically, in which the company might be said to be post-modern is in the image it projects of itself (Bryman 1995: 194). Walt Disney is painted as a visionary who cared little about money but wished upon a star, animators whistle while they work, and rank-and-file cast members go off to work with a hearty 'hi-ho'. None of it is true, but it serves to disguise the political economy of a profit-maximizing capitalist enterprise.

Postmodernism is characterized by a penchant for pastiche, an ironic, self-parodying stance that facilitates the knowing consumption of kitsch. The parks embody time-space compression (Harvey 1989), bringing together collages of items drawn from different cultures at different time periods. Walt Disney's aim was to create a magical realm outside the familiar coordinates of time and space. Much of what is offered are, in Baudrillard's terms, *simulacra* – faithful copies of entities that never existed, for example Mickey Mouse and Donald Duck. Bryman points out that there are precedents for all this in the great exhibitions of the nineteenth century; Disney is drawing on a long tradition, not inventing something from scratch. Historical continuity is at least as striking as cultural innovation.

Dedifferentiation of consumption is one of the defining characteristics of Disneyization. But what of the postmodern dedifferentiation of reality and appearance? Is a Disney park a hyperreality constructed of simulacra? And have we reached the point, as Baudrillard (1983) suggests, where Disney worlds are the reality that America is emulating?

A recurrent criticism is that Disney wilfully distorts history, erasing painful memories and supplying in their place sentimental nostalgia for a mythic past and mindless celebration of a technologically driven future. The possible defence, that Disney is about entertainment and fun, is undercut by its self-confessed educational thrust. Disney's commodification of history has the depressing outcome that the consumer's appetite for genuine historical study is not whetted but sated (Wallace 1996: 170). How could it be otherwise, given where the money is coming from? The contradiction, Wallace argues, is not between education and entertainment, but between critical history and the commercial interests of Disney and its corporate partners.

Bryman concedes that distinguishing between real and fake can sometimes be a problem for the visitor. It is not too difficult to pick out the audio-animatronic figures (the talking robots) from the cast members (the employees), but other features of the landscape and the habitat are not so easily identified. Occasional momentary dislocations, common enough in other fields – as he is dragged unexpectedly off the stage, has the Shakespearean actor been injured in the sword fight? – do not amount to the collapse of reality and appearance into a hyperreality.

This leads on to the most problematic questions of all: what do the visitors make of all this? Why are they there, and what do they take away from it other than an assortment of Disney merchandise? Here it does make a good deal of sense to see the visitors as 'post-tourists' (Bryman 1995: 174–9; Rojek 1993: 177). Post-tourists are unconcerned about the commodification of experiences; theirs is an ironic posture, not a serious-minded search for authenticity. They do not care that events are staged, so long are they are staged professionally – as they are at Disney, where technical competence is unsurpassed. Post-tourists treat tourist experiences as ends in themselves. They delight in the array of spectacular signs set out before them, including the merchandise (gifts for family and friends) and the company of their fellow tourists.

The term 'post-tourist' is, I would argue, misleading. It appears to reify a mode of consumption into a state of being. Being a post-tourist on some occasions does not rule out a search for authenticity on others. In Britain, the recently opened gallery of contemporary art, Tate Modern, has proved a success with a wide public, despite the 'difficult' material it displays. At the same time, the Millennium Dome, with its displays of sponsored mediocrity, ended in fiasco.

People who visit Disney theme parks and other cathedrals of consumption are not pilgrims who wish to return home transformed or cured; instead, they are looking for diversion and recreation, a welcome relief from pressing everyday realities of home and especially work. Who is to say that this is not rational?

Globalization and cross-cultural consumption

McDonaldization and Disneyization: do these processes represent the global triumph of Western capitalism, a hollowing out of local cultures and their replacement by the fetishism of commodities – in short, cultural imperialism? Although the globalization of culture might be seen as liberating the Third World into a worldwide society of affluence, freedom, democracy and universal human rights, most critics have drawn the more pessimistic conclusion that globalization means cultural homogenization. Tomlinson offers a striking metaphor (1999: 83): international airports may be gateways to cultural diversity, but their retail areas contain nothing but a standardized array of global cultural icons and brands.

Yet there is a strong case for arguing, against the extreme optimist and the extreme pessimist, that the lived realities of globalized culture are significantly different from the former's dreams and the latter's nightmares. Both optimists and pessimists treat indigenous cultures as the passive subjects of Western cultural imperialism, leaping too hastily from 'the simple presence of cultural goods to the attribution of deeper cultural or ideological effects' (Tomlinson 1999: 84). Flattening out the complex relationships between societies, both optimists and pessimists overstate the power of the West and underestimate the capacity of other cultures to resist it. It is admittedly increasingly hard for nation-states to regulate the activities of transnational corporations, monitor and control flows of migrant labour, or even prevent imports of undesired commodities. None of this demonstrates the thesis of global cultural homogeneity.

A more profitable approach to the analysis of consumption that crosses the cultural boundaries of nation-states is suggested by an analogy with the development of language: the process of creolization (Howes 1996: 5–8). When cultures come into contact, they often devise a makeshift language, technically called a pidgin, which facilitates trading relationships between them, including master–slave relations. Pidgins have simple grammar and a limited vocabulary geared specifically to commerce and drawn mainly from the superstrate language (the language of the dominant partner). As culture contact develops, pidgins typically evolve into a hybrid language spoken by children as their mother tongue, which then becomes the language of the indigenous culture. Technically, a pidgin has evolved into a creole.

Applied to culture more generally, the concept of creolization underlines the richness of cultural hybrids and the creative energy of cultures which do not simply receive Western commodities but transform them. Even the mightiest global brands are subject to creolization. Prendergrast (1993) points out that Coca-Cola, surely a ready-made symbol of unstoppable cultural imperialism, has been appropriated as a cosmetic that can smooth wrinkles (Russia), as having the alchemical property of turning copper into silver (Barbados), and as a potion that can revive the dead (Haiti).

Nor is cultural exchange a one-way traffic from the West to the rest. To regard the West as non-permeable by other cultures is to adopt a crude stereotype of the West itself (Classen and Howes 1996: 188–91). Goods from the non-Western 'other' are consumed as hybrids. A well-known symbol of this in the UK is the popular curry, Chicken Tikka Masala, a dish unknown on the Indian subcontinent. It may be worth adding that most self-styled 'Indian' restaurants are owned not by Hindus from India but by Muslims from Bangladesh and Pakistan.

Discussion of creolization suggests another metaphor drawn from the evolution of language: the Latin analogy. Latin is a 'dead' language, one that has ceased to be the mother tongue of any language community. Yet Latin – not in its pure classical form as practised by the great Roman poets, historians, playwrights and orators, but the 'vulgar' Latin spoken by the common people – evolved into the Romance languages, including French, Italian, Spanish, Catalan, Portuguese and Romanian. Is today's world language, English, destined for the same future, becoming a set of related languages that are not mutually comprehensible? If so, it would not be a victory for global linguistic homogenization, but a defeat.

The McDonaldization thesis presents itself as a critical assault on the iron, velvet and rubber cages of rationalization. Paradoxically, the thesis can also serve to glorify the achievements of transnational corporations, providing a theorized rationale of their supposed global dominance. In that perspective, it may be argued that McDonaldization is a myth that serves the interests of McDonald's.

6

Consumer Activism

The scope of consumer rights

In 1962, US President John F. Kennedy presented a message to Congress in which he identified what came to be known as 'the consumer's Bill of Rights'. His underlying theme was that the pace of social and technological change had made it harder for people to evaluate the array of goods and services on offer. New laws were needed to enshrine four basic consumer rights:

- *The right to safety*: to be protected against the marketing of goods hazardous to health or life.
- *The right to be informed*: to be protected against fraudulent, deceitful or grossly misleading information, advertising, labelling, or other practices, and to be given the facts needed to make an informed choice.
- *The right to choose*: to be assured, wherever possible, of access to a variety of products and services at competitive prices; and in those industries in which competition is not workable and government regulation is substituted, an assurance of satisfactory quality and service at fair prices.
- *The right to be heard*: to be assured that the consumer interest will receive full and sympathetic consideration in

the formulation of government policy, and fair and expeditious treatment in administrative tribunals.

Kennedy's approach presupposed an affluent First World society with a competitive free market economy through which citizens' basic needs had already been met. He called for legislation not to distort market mechanisms but to set them free. What the consumer wants, and what Kennedy aimed to support, was value for money.

Since 1962, pressure groups have argued for an extension of consumer rights beyond the four set out in Kennedy's speech. Consumers International proposes four more consumer rights:

- *The right to redress*: to receive a fair settlement of just claims, including compensation for misrepresentation, shoddy goods or unsatisfactory services. The right to redress is a strengthening of Kennedy's right to be heard. Government must do more than listen; it must act. Furthermore, redress is needed not just against public bodies but also against private sector organizations.
- *The right to consumer education*: to acquire knowledge and skills needed to make informed, confident choices about goods and services, while being aware of basic consumer rights and responsibilities and how to act on them. The right to consumer education is an extension of Kennedy's right to be informed. Supplying people with information is effective only if they have the cultural capital necessary to understand it.

The rights to redress and to consumer education imply a more politically active consumer, one who has been educated to assert her rights and to demand compensation if they are violated. The passive concept of consumer protection is not enough; consumers need to be empowered. The remaining new rights are an even more significant departure from Kennedy's vision.

- *The right to a healthy environment*: to live and work in an environment which is not threatening to the well-being of present and future generations. This right addresses the potential conflict between producers and consumers, and between present and future generations. It implies that the price mechanism of a free market is not adequate to the task of sustaining the environment now and for the future.

- *The right to satisfaction of basic needs*: to have access to basic, essential goods and services such as adequate food, clothing, shelter, health care, education, public utilities, water and sanitation. This right confronts the problem of social inequality within and between nations – which takes us well beyond the preoccupations of value-for-money consumerism.

Yet another consumer right has been put forward: *the right to privacy*. The massive potential for storage, retrieval and manipulation of electronic data has given rise to legislation designed to offer protection against abuse of privacy. In the 1970s, the United States formulated six fundamental principles of privacy for the computer age (Loudon and Della Bitta 1993: 640):

- Only relevant and socially approved personal information should be collected by private or public organizations seeking to determine people's access to rights, benefits, and opportunities.
- Individuals should be told what information about them is to be collected and how it will be used.
- Individuals should have practical procedures for inspecting their records and for raising issues as to the accuracy, completeness, and propriety of information used to make evaluative decisions about them.
- Sensitive personal information should be circulated within the collecting organization only to those with a need to see it for legitimate purposes.
- Disclosures of identified personal information should not be made by collecting organizations to others outside the original area of activity unless agreed to by the individual or required by legal process.
- Organizations must create and apply effective data security measures so that they can keep the promises of confidentiality that they have made to individuals whose information they are holding in a trustee relationship.

The range of rights outlined above shows some of the difficulties in defining consumer rights and delimiting their scope. Equally problematic is the question, how can consumer rights best be protected? Three possibilities can be distinguished: by the free market, by the state, and by voluntary organizations.

Laissez-faire: the market as guarantor of consumer rights

Advocates of the free market are typically sceptical about claims of market failure, as we saw in chapter 3 (pp. 59–64 above). Some even argue that *all* market failure is mythical. Although they vary in how far they take their advocacy of the free market, all agree that intervention has unintended consequences that tend to subvert the aims of those proposing it.

Meddling with the market is perilous even when the goal is consumer protection. For example, rationing scarce commodities in times of national emergency might appear to be an excellent policy. In a total war, civilians need to pull together in a common purpose despite inequalities of status and wealth. Rationing appears to be the way to ensure fairness and boost morale. Instead of using the socially divisive price mechanism, goods are allocated by benevolent administrative decisions. Nobody starves, and everyone is fit to contribute to the war effort.

But with what result? If quantities are rationed and prices kept artificially low, consumers who gain little benefit from a good will use it wastefully. Worse, producers will have no economic incentive to increase supply, which will create an unnecessary shortage. As for staple goods such as basic foodstuffs and fuel, consumers will buy excess quantities in order to build up a stockpile to anticipate shortages. A black market will develop, where goods are offered illegally at prices higher than the official level, producing greater inequality than under a market system, encouraging corruption and rewarding crime. Scarce goods will be kept 'under the counter' and allocated to favoured customers according to the prejudices of the retailer (drily referred to in the literature as 'sellers' preferences'). The civilian population is placed at the mercy of butchers and grocers. Administering the system will inevitably create generous employment for bureaucrats, at enormous but uncalculated cost.

Regulation is very efficient at one thing – breeding bureaucracy. Individuals and private companies face high compliance costs. Regulators have an interest in keeping the regulatory system going, and therefore in formulating ever more complex rules which they alone can understand and administer. They claim to have 'a light touch', but seldom do. Efforts to simplify the system have little effect – witness the seemingly inevitable impenetrability of income tax forms throughout the civilized world.

'Regulatory capture' is one of the dangers inherent in institutions set up to protect consumers from incompetence and fraud. It occurs when regulators identify too closely with the interests of the industry or sector they are charged with regulating. Regulators may equate the public interest with the interests of producers rather than consumers. The recognition that there may be lucrative job opportunities in the firms being regulated is one reason why regulators may be captured – they ingratiate themselves with people who can offer them a better job. Environmental protection agencies, for example, cannot compete with salaries in the oil industry.

Consumer protection, like insurance, carries the risk that people will behave recklessly because they are assured of compensation when things go wrong. People take excessive risks, and if things go badly for them they expect other taxpayers to bail them out. This 'moral hazard' arises when people have an incentive to behave in ways which generate costs that others have to bear. Moral hazard can encourage corruption – for instance, conspiring to commit arson in order to cash in on insurance policies.

Most free marketeers acknowledge that there are situations in which the market fails to deliver adequate protection to the consumer. Some consumers are particularly vulnerable, and there are circumstances in which virtually everyone needs a cushion of legislation to uphold their rights as consumers.

The state as upholder of consumer rights

Protecting vulnerable people is a common rationale for consumer protection. Definitions of who is most at risk vary historically and cross-culturally. Here, for example, are seven categories of vulnerable consumer recognized by the Office of Fair Trading in England and Wales: people on low income, the unemployed, people suffering from long-term illness or disability, people with low educational attainment, members of ethnic minorities, older people, and young people (Scott and Black 2000: 4–8). In Bourdieu's terms, these people tend to have relatively low levels of economic, cultural and social capital. Their lack of economic capital means that the cost of poor goods and services is one they cannot easily absorb. They also lack the cultural capital that would leave them better placed to evaluate goods and services, and the social capital that would provide them with reliable objective advice.

Consumer protection goes further than protecting vulnerable consumers; it also protects everyone in situations where most of us are vulnerable. This is true of many services, and also when we are confronted with so-called *credence goods*. There are many situations where we cannot easily assess the quality of the good or service on offer, and have to take it on trust: when they are technically complex; when we purchase them infrequently and so lack experience and accumulated wisdom; when problems are likely to emerge only after several years; and when they are private affairs that people seldom discuss in public.

If our experience and education count for very little, we may be obliged to turn to professionals for their expert advice. The growth of the knowledge-based professions is deeply embedded in the rise of consumer society. Markets operate on the principle of *caveat emptor* (let the buyer beware), whereas professional–client relations are based on the principle of *credat emptor* – let the buyer believe. Many of the scandals of consumer society involve a breach by professionals of their position of trust.

If self-regulation by professional bodies fails to satisfy the imperatives of consumer protection, the state typically intervenes to impose a regulatory framework within which professionals are required to operate.

Although state intervention in the marketplace can give rise to accusations of an interfering 'nanny state', it can also be popular. States need to gain legitimacy in the eyes of their members, winning respect and active commitment that go beyond mere compliance (Habermas 1973). The state's role in consumer protection is a powerful mechanism for gaining legitimacy. This applies not just in obvious cases such as legislation against inferior services, shoddy goods and fraud. Consumer protection has been extended to deal, for example, with despised religious movements – the 'cults'. They are charged not with heresy but with a variety of secular offences such as breaking up families, brainwashing, mind control, financial extortion and sexual abuse. They are regularly accused of preying on people who are immature, emotionally unstable or mentally ill.

States profess to act on behalf of consumers, but the claim deserves to be received sceptically. Consumer protection is often more top-down than bottom-up, a point Burgess (2001) illustrates through the example of the European Union. Consumer protection has been ratcheted up, so that measures to promote the consumer interest are seldom rejected as excessive. The EU has moved decisively towards a risk-averse, precautionary approach, acting to limit damage for fear of the worst case scenario. This approach is most evident in cases of scientific and technological innovation. The BSE crisis was a turning point in consolidating the precautionary approach, which is now manifest in the EU's policy on genetically modified food. In the name of empowerment, so Burgess's argument runs, the precautionary approach constitutes the consumer as a victim who cannot attend to his or her own interests without the state's 'help'.

The institutions of the European Union are frequently criticized as undemocratic and excessively bureaucratic. Perhaps they hope to gain legitimacy through championing consumer rights, but it is a risky game. Their protection may be seen as patronizing meddling. Since anthropologists have emphasized the significance of urban myths, it is worth noting two entrenched British myths about the EU's attempts at consumer protection. Brussels bureaucrats are widely believed to favour legislation requiring all bananas to be straight (a denial of the facts of nature), and banning the British sausage (an affront to British culture).

Consumer organizations and value for money

At first sight, the aims of consumer organizations such as the UK's *Consumers' Association* and the US *Consumer Union* appear straightforward. Their mission is twofold: to supply consumers with objective information, gathered through comparative tests of goods and services, that will enable them to make a rational choice and obtain value for money; and to lobby the government for legislation to uphold consumer rights. As a guarantee of their objectivity, consumer organizations stay independent from the state, commercial organizations and other pressure groups. They accept neither subsidies from government nor advertising and sponsorship from private enterprise, relying instead on sales of magazines, books and services to their members.

Consumer organizations originated in the Fordist era and, as Sassatelli observes (1995: 18), had their heyday in the late 1960s and early 1970s – just when Fordism was playing out its endgame. Consumer organization depended on mass production and product standardization. If products are not standardized but variable or customized, the strategy of selecting a small sample of goods for comparative testing would be pointless, since no generalization could be made from it. If they depend on mass production to make their research methodology meaningful, consumer organizations also depend on a mass market of consumers for their own publications and services. Magazines like the UK's *Which?* and France's *Que choisir?* are aimed at a general readership – 'the consumer' – not at specialists or connoisseurs.

The primary source of their objective information is controlled laboratory experiments, in which products are subjected to a series of tests to measure performance, reliability and durability. A second source of information is independent scientific and professional experts, who may be called upon to judge the technical specifications of complex products and services. Finally, consumer organizations conduct surveys of their members. These surveys gather

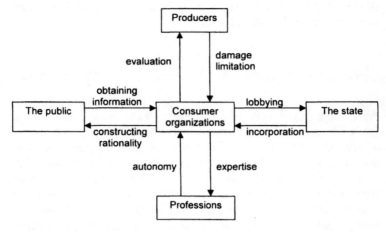

Figure 6.1 Consumer organizations in the field of consumption

factual data about the performance of consumer goods, the incidence of faults and the cost of repairs. Interestingly, *facts* about goods are more important to consumer organizations than the *opinions* of consumers, because opinion is merely subjective.

Consumer publications aim to identify the 'best' buys that have the most favourable ratio of price to performance. The claim is that they will save the readers money. Taken together with their lobbying for consumer rights, the mission of consumer organizations is, then, *to prevent consumers from becoming victims, and to enable them to be well-informed rational actors.*

In pursuit of this mission, consumer organizations are enmeshed in a network of interrelations with other stakeholders in the field of consumer protection and consumer rights, as set out in figure 6.1.

Consumer organizations and producers

There are obvious tensions here. Consumer reports would lose their rationale if they failed to identify 'best buys'. They need to quantify their results, awarding stars, or a location on a scale from best to worst, or points out of ten or a hundred. At the same time, consumer organizations want to preserve their impartiality, and so strive to prevent manufacturers and service providers from using their recommendations as product endorsements ('as recommended by *Which?*').

If there are best buys there are also worst buys. Consumer organizations need a professionally staffed legal department to protect themselves against the threat of litigation by companies alleging that their goods and services have been misrepresented. All consumer organizations have the potential to publish damaging copy about the performance and safety of the items they scrutinize. The best known of these was Ralph Nader's scathing 1960s campaign against American car manufacturers that were blatantly disregarding safety in pursuit of profit (Gartman 1994: 208–11). Nader famously chose the Chevrolet Corvair as a case study of an automobile that was 'unsafe at any speed' because of the faulty design of its rear suspension, a problem known to General Motors executives before the car was launched. Having failed to find anything discreditable in Nader's private life, and faced with incontrovertible evidence that he had his facts right, GM was forced to apologize to him and pay $425,000 in settlement of a civil law suit. It was a dramatic demonstration of the power of organized consumerism over even the mightiest corporation. Since this landmark case, corporations have tended to adopt more subtle ways of limiting the damage caused by adverse consumer reports.

Consumer organizations and the state

Although they are studiously non-partisan, consumer organizations are always campaigning for legislation to be enacted or extended in order to protect consumers against shoddy goods and inadequate services. Consumer reports are regularly featured in newspapers and broadcast media, particularly when they expose scandals.

The state's obvious strategy is to try to incorporate consumer organizations into regulatory institutions (Burgess

2001). Incorporation will make it harder for consumer organizations to criticize failures of regulation, and their involvement as consumer advocates will help to legitimize the regulatory bodies. Consumer organizations can acquire a quasi-official status that may damage their independence. They also face the problem of an insatiable demand by the state for their expert evidence and advice, which may strain their capacity to supply it.

Consumer organizations and the professions

Before the 1980s, consumer organizations focused on comparative testing of manufactured products. In response to the growing significance of the service sector, they now devote more and more attention to services, including maintenance and repair of consumer goods and advice from professionals. The question is, how to carry out the equivalent of a controlled laboratory experiment on car servicing or financial advice? The answer is to use undercover investigators, who present themselves incognito to the service provider and book their car in for a service or seek advice on how to invest for their children's education.

To bring about the equivalent of a controlled experiment, the investigator's car has to be pre-prepared with a set of faults which the garage ought to identify and put right. Similarly, the investigator seeking financial advice needs to be supplied with a set script giving details about salient facts such as their health, occupation, family responsibilities, financial objectives and attitude to risk. To prepare the car, and to write the script, consumer organizations employ independent professional experts. These professionals will then judge the quality of the work and advice of their fellow professionals.

The findings of such investigations are invariably an indictment of professional advisers. I have yet to read a *Which?* report on any profession that has not emphasized widespread and serious lapses of professional judgement and conduct. Professions respond partly by objecting to the deceptive nature of undercover investigation, and partly by arguing that professional advice has to be tailored to the needs of individual clients, cannot be standardized, and is therefore inescapably a matter of judgement. Consumer organizations, they claim, betray a misplaced Fordism by insisting on simple uniform solutions to complex individual problems.

The relationship between consumer organizations and the professions is ambivalent. On the one hand, consumer organizations are a scourge of professional malpractice, but at the same time they depend on professionals for knowledge and expertise. Consumer organizations uphold the ideals of professionalism, taking a strikingly romantic view of them. Professionals and professional associations are attacked not for an excess of professionalism but for a lack of it. Despite the surface antagonism there is, therefore, what Bourdieu calls an 'objective complicity' between consumer organizations and the professions. They are in the same game and they need each other.

Consumer organizations and the public

What appears to be a straightforward relationship is arguably the most problematic. Consumers want objective information, and consumer organizations supply it. What could be simpler?

The project of consumer organizations is to constitute the consumer as a rational actor. This means that consumers must be persuaded to adopt a set of character virtues: to be goal-oriented, forward-looking, disciplined, consistent of purpose, and frugal. They must display, in other words, this-worldly asceticism, the Weberian Protestant ethic (A. Aldridge 1994). Hence the publications produced by consumer organizations represent consumption as *work*. There is, or should be, nothing frivolous about it. 'Retail therapy' is not a concept that consumer organizations are willing to endorse.

All acts of consumption are subject to the scrutiny of consumer organizations, so that even minor purchases such as a toothbrush or a saucepan are put through carefully controlled laboratory experiments. Critics who see these items as too trivial to be worthy of attention miss the point. When an organization's mission is character building, everything counts. Consumers must be constantly reminded of their duty to be rational in all their acts of consumption.

It follows that consumer organizations do far more than supply objective information about how to get value for money. Their mission is to fashion consumer culture as a sphere of rational action undertaken by this-worldly ascetics. In the UK, the point can be illustrated by the failure of the monthly magazine, *Check It Out!* Launched by the Consumers' Association in September 1992, it folded barely a year later. The key reason it failed was that it used the apparatus and philosophy of the main magazine, *Which?*, but targeted it at ten- to fifteen-year-olds. The ideals of rational consumption were poorly received by an audience of style-conscious adolescents.

Consumer organizations' approach to consumption attempts the impossible: to strip consumption practices from their socio-cultural context. Laboratory tests, panels of experts, incognito investigators with a predefined script: all these methodologies are artificially abstracted from naturally occurring social interaction. Perhaps the supreme example is the 'blind test'. Scientific studies have demonstrated that if they are placed in an experimental situation where they do not know which product they are consuming, most people are unable to identify their favourite brands. Accepting these findings, what conclusion should be drawn? To consumer organizations it is obvious: if you cannot tell the difference, buy the cheapest product and save yourself money. In real life, however, people *can* see the packaging, the label and the logo, so they and the people they interact with know that the beer is Budweiser, the perfume is Dior and the trainers are Reebok. We may wish it were not so, but – at least under capitalism – it is.

Artificially engineered blind tests demonstrate the folly of trying to strip consumption from its context. Real life settings also show the problem of determining a context-free objective reality. Consider the common experience of bringing home wine we have enjoyed on a summer holiday abroad. Consumed on a wet Sunday afternoon in a grey northern country, what we thought was a characterful Chianti from the hills of Tuscany now tastes, frankly, rough. Should we conclude that the pleasure of being on holiday made it seem better than it really was, or that there is nothing wrong with the wine other than the dreary Sunday afternoon and the dispiriting prospect of returning to work on Monday? Taking another holiday in Tuscany to try the wine again cannot resolve this question – though it might be a good move anyway.

Because consumer organizations cannot easily handle the symbolic aspects of consumption, they try to minimize their significance. To magazines like *Which?*, taste is a private matter on which they cannot comment. The claim to 'bracket off' any consideration of aesthetics is a futile attempt to suppress the expressive dimension – the scale running from communicator to dupe.

Ethics, too, are treated as a private idiosyncrasy. If you want to invest ethically, this fund is good value – but if not, then *this other one*, which admittedly invests in union-busting companies, armaments manufacturers and oppressive regimes, is a star performer and a best buy. If you are concerned for the environment, then this is the most energy-efficient washing machine; but if you are not 'green' then *this other one* is cheaper and gets your clothes cleaner.

In failing to address the environmental impact of consumption, consumer organizations show a schizoid denial of the future, and in failing to address the ethics of consumption, they show a schizoid denial of production. Perhaps they cannot face the bad news? Paradoxically, it is not consumers but consumer organizations that display symptoms of narcissism.

Beyond value for money: confronting consumers with producers

Naomi Klein's *No Logo* (2000) can be read as a commentary on the limitations of old-style value-for-money consumerism.

Klein begins with the crucial claim that brands are not what they were. Originally, brands were a guarantee of product quality, a guarantee that people need in a mobile, urbanized, impersonal society. No longer able to rely on personal recommendations from trusted retailers (see chapter 2, pp. 35–6), consumers began to put their faith in brand names and were rational to do so. Companies invest heavily in brands, and so have had an interest in maintaining quality. If a brand acquires a poor reputation consumers will desert it, and the company will have wasted a huge investment. Because brands have carried an inbuilt guarantee of quality, consumers have been prepared to pay a premium price for them.

All this is changing, according to Klein. Drawing many of her examples from the world of fashion, she argues that brands such as Nike, Adidas, Reebok, Tommy Hilfiger, Gucci and Armani are not about quality or reliability, but lifestyle. When consumer organizations put them through laboratory tests these brands do not perform especially well – but that is not the point. The brand has been uncoupled from the product, so product testing is irrelevant.

The ascendancy of lifestyle brands and the corporations that nurture them has profound effects. Brands are 'branded' in a number of ways.

As anti-competitive   Lifestyle brands are a feature of globalized monopoly capitalism. Transnational corporations have shared interests, including the need to suppress competition. Ronald Reagan's neoliberal administration relaxed US anti-trust laws, making mergers between large corporations easier to achieve, while at the same time tightening the laws on copyright and trade marks. Greater licence was given to corporate intimidation of independent traders, such as the Illinois restaurateur whose real name is Ronald McDonald, and who found himself sued by McDonald's on behalf of their clown.

As exploitative   The corporations whose business is lifestyle brands typically offer insecure, non-union, casualized employment. Manufacture is contracted out to Third World sweatshops, places where taxes, labour unions and labour regulations do not reach.

As anti-democratic   The omnipresence of brands, and their litigious suppression of all opposition or even playful appropriation of logos and slogans, stifles free speech and democracy. Public spaces become private, as in shopping malls with their private security forces. The ultimate irony, with which Klein ends her book, is the development of corporate codes of conduct. Drafted by public relations departments with no input from workers or unions, these pseudo-manifestos of human rights – Klein calls them 'hybrids of advertising copy and the Communist Manifesto' (2000: 431) – are potentially lethal to citizenship. 'When we start looking to corporations to draft our collective labour and human rights codes for us' she concludes, 'we have already lost the most basic principle of citizenship: that people should govern themselves' (2000: 441).

The subtitle of Klein's book is *Taking aim at the brand bullies*. But what weapons can be used, and will they find their target? It seems clear that, on her argument, value-for-money consumerism is irrelevant. Its insistence on the instrumental aspect of consumption, and its silence on the communicator–dupe axis – not least its bracketing of aesthetics and ethics – mean that it poses little threat to corporations and their brands. The Puritan values of consumer organizations may expose them to ridicule as self-righteous killjoys.

Ridicule is, conversely, a weapon against the brands. Cultural jammers and adbusters parody advertisements mercilessly, aiming for a killer countermessage that will subvert the corporation's carefully nurtured brand images. An example is Joe Camel, the friendly cartoon animal depicted on packets of Camel cigarettes. In the hands of the adbusters he became the ravaged Joe Chemo, battling with lung cancer. Corporations may find it hard to fight back against destructive images of this kind, for fear that they will alienate the public and merely reinforce the unwanted message in the minds of their consumers. On the other hand, adbusting may be no more than merry pranksterism, amounting merely to fun for those who take part. Corporations can capture the pranksters, since an obvious career move for Klein's 'semiotic Robin Hoods' is to become semiotic Sheriffs of Nottingham. Thus Nike approached the consumer champion Ralph Nader and offered him $25,000 to endorse Air 120 trainers with the slogan: 'Another shameless attempt by Nike to sell shoes' (Klein 2000: 302). He refused.

Brands, as argued above, are complicit with value-for-money consumerism in occluding the production process. One way in which brands may therefore be challenged is to confront consumers with the grim truths of production, such as union busting, testing of products on animals, and sweatshops. The attempted confrontation may not work, since perhaps only a minority of middle-class consumers will respond to attempts to make them feel guilty about their purchases and their lifestyle.

Brands may nevertheless be more vulnerable than they appear. Brand 'loyalty' is scarcely secure: modern corporations are not, as they might wish, objects of unquestioning adulation, and few people find the meaning of life in trainers or a sweatshirt. Economic recession may be enough to puncture the pretensions of this elite wing of the rag trade.

Consumer activism in the age of promotional culture

In an incisive critique of consumer society, Wernick (1991) coins the term 'promotional culture'. His thesis is that 'the range of cultural phenomena which, at least as one of their functions, serve to communicate a promotional message has become, today, virtually co-extensive with our produced symbolic world' (1991: 182). No form of communication is shielded from the advancement of individual and corporate self-interest. Advertising has broken free from the confines of the advertisement. Promotional culture blurs the boundaries between editorials and advertisements, education and entertainment, fact and fiction. New words have been invented – advertorials, edutainment, faction – betraying the corrosion of the old distinctions.

Promotion is neither simply decorative (advertising puff – which we can ignore) nor dissimulating (passing one thing off as something else – but we need not be fooled). Promotion changes the very nature of goods and services. Use-value is swallowed up by exchange-value, so that 'an object which happens to circulate is converted into one which is designed to do so' (Wernick 1991:190). This is to restate the Frankfurt School's concern with the commodification of culture. Since we become commodities ourselves, the problem is personal as well as political; for if, as Wernick claims, social survival depends on perpetually attuning our performances to an audience, 'what are we behind the mask?' (1991: 93).

In a parallel argument, Klein speaks of a 'third culture' that fuses corporations and the culture they brand. Business corporations are ever more successful in colonizing the culture of First World societies. The neoliberal project to roll back the state and encourage private enterprise has left public sector organizations starved of resources. They need corporate sponsors if they are to remain solvent. This is also true of 'mega-events' (Roche 2000) such as the Olympics or the World Cup. The balance of power has changed, according to Klein (2000: 31–6). In the past, sponsored events involved a fair exchange: the cultural institution received some welcome cash, and the corporate sponsor benefited from publicity and a tax break. The event remained authentic, and sponsors gained credit from being associated with it. But corporations have become progressively more demanding, and cultural organizations more enslaved by them. Events are usurped and drained of their authenticity, so that participants feel their event has been appropriated, as indeed it has.

Klein's analysis suggests that organized consumerism may not be able to resist the colonization of culture by the corporations. She focuses on the power of sponsorship, but surprisingly neglects a more insidious practice. Product placement, also known as embedded advertising, is the practice whereby a company offers payment or other incentives to have a product, or an advertisement for a product, appear in a television drama or cinema film as if it were a 'natural' element in the story-line. Organized consumerism has shown itself powerless to contest the incursions of product placement.

The earliest example of product placement can be dated to 1886, the year in which a private company purchased the painting by Sir John Everett Millais, *Bubbles*. This canvas depicts an innocent-looking boy with golden curls, who is blowing soap bubbles using a child's clay pipe. The company paid Millais a fee for the rights to reproduce the picture. In return, the artist agreed that the painting would be retouched to include in the foreground a bar of Pears' soap.

Product placement was common even in the early years of the motion picture industry. Cash-strapped film producers were grateful for props supplied by commercial companies. As the industry developed the practice became endemic, and more sophisticated. Almost a century after *Bubbles*, the James Bond films were a rich outlet for product placement. The first major example of a branded item in a James Bond film was the Aston Martin sports car featured in *Goldfinger*. This was not, surprisingly, an example of product placement. Aston Martin was afraid that association with a mass-market film would sully its luxury image, but agreed reluctantly to *sell* three cars to the film company. Times changed rapidly, and James Bond films became famous for the conspicuous display of Omega watches, Samsonite luggage, Church's shoes and Calvin Klein sunglasses. When Bond temporarily switched from Aston Martin to BMW, it was an undeniable coup for the German manufacturer.

Flaunting up-market consumer goods was at least faithful to the spirit of the original novels. Ian Fleming's James Bond stories are full of references to branded goods that signal the affluent, socially exclusive circles in which 007 operated. They may have been intended to bring aspirational colour into the drab lives of Fleming's readers. What, though, if a story is written explicitly in order to promote branded goods? In *Murder in Small Town X*, a television mystery series launched in the United States in 2001, a remarkable number of the central characters were portrayed driving DaimlerChrysler Jeeps, dining in Taco Bell restaurants, ordering Pepsi, and talking to one another on Nokia mobile phones (Drummond 2001). These corporations were, of course, funding the programmes. Arguably, their products had ceased to be mere props and were now part of the story.

An analysis of the most profitable Hollywood films of 1990 (Wasko et al. 1993) shows the extent of product placement. *Ghost* featured sixteen brands, *Teenage Mutant Ninja Turtles* eighteen, *Pretty Woman* twenty, *Total Recall* twenty-eight, and *Home Alone* thirty-one. This reflects the success not only of the corporations themselves, but also of product placement agencies acting on behalf of them. Such agencies often represent a 'family' of products, which they try to place as a package deal.

Hollywood films reach an international market, as do most but not all branded goods and services. In the futuristic film *Demolition Man*, only one fast-food chain has survived. Sylvester Stallone's words in the American release of the film are: 'Taco Bell', the US-based TexMex chain. Outside the US, the soundtrack has been dubbed: 'Pizza Hut' (Fowles 1996: 147n). It may well be that new technologies offer further opportunities for tailoring product placement to national requirements.

In 2001, the author Fay Weldon published a novel commissioned by the Italian jewellery firm, Bulgari. She undertook to include at least twelve references to Bulgari's merchandise. *The Bulgari Connection* provoked critical strictures on the author's alleged breach of artistic integrity. Against this, it might be said that the nature of Fay Weldon's novel was publicized well in advance, that the whole affair had a strong vein of self-parody, and that she did not aspire to win any literary prizes. The question is: does this mitigate the dangers of embedded persuasion, or is it a subtle expression of them? Does irony protect us from exploitation or deliver us over to it?

If the United States is comparatively relaxed about product placement, the regulatory authorities in other countries have struggled to uphold the independence and integrity of programme producers, and to restrict the scope of commercial influence over programme content (Murdock 1992). In the United Kingdom there are at the time of writing three key regulators, but it is proposed to merge them into one. Public sector television and radio are subject to Producers' Guidelines drawn up by the BBC and overseen by a Board of Governors; these guidelines are available on the web at www.bbc.co.uk/info/editorial/prodgl/index.shtml. Commercial television is regulated (as at April 2002) by the Independent Television Commission, and commercial radio by the Radio Authority (www.radioauthority.org.uk).

Product placement is not allowed in UK television and radio programmes. Even so, the regulators concede that branded goods may well be necessary to portray contemporary life realistically. It is one thing for a character in the long-running radio soap opera about rural life, *The Archers*, to ask the landlord of The Bull for 'a pint of Shires'; but such playful fictions will hardly do in serious television drama. Dirty realism demands real dirt. Justified on the grounds of dramatic realism, product placement can lead to absurdity, as when everybody drinks Miller beer and no other brand is in sight. One possibility is to rotate brands, as in the detergents used in the UK television soap opera *EastEnders* by characters patronizing the local launderette (Murdock 1992: 226). However the issue of realism is treated, an important consequence is a bias towards depicting contemporary life. It is hard to envisage *David Copperfield* or *Pride and Prejudice* as vehicles of product placement.

Acknowledging the demands of dramatic realism, the response of the independent Television Commission is to enforce the principle that commercial products and services must not be given 'undue prominence' (ITC 2002: 44). No impression must be given of outside commercial influence on the editorial process, even if none has been exerted. The camera should not dwell on branded goods, which should not be shown in close-up or from an angle that highlights the brand image. Preferably, labels and logos should be turned away from the cameras.

A typical example of the ITC's work is the case of the Channel 5 programme, *5 News*, which carried an item on seasonal affective disorder (ITC 2001). The film contained a sequence in which a nurse was shown getting ready to go to work, and preparing herself a cup of coffee. There were two close-ups, each three seconds long, of a jar of Douwe Egberts coffee, with the commentary: 'Even her special blend of black coffee and the most irritating local radio breakfast show she can find fails to force her out of the house on time.' One viewer complained that this sequence gave undue prominence to the Douwe Egberts brand. Channel 5 argued that the word 'special' merely emphasized that the coffee, though strong and black, could not shake the nurse out of her torpor. The ITC disagreed. It found that the close-ups of the coffee jar gave undue prominence to the brand, and that referring to the nurse's 'special blend' indicated her brand preference.

Although the ITC accepted that the programme makers had not been influenced by external commercial pressures, it found that the close-ups and the script gave the impression of product placement, and were therefore in breach of the Programme Code. This trivial example, chosen arbitrarily from among countless others, illustrates the routine work of regulatory agencies battling, it may be hopelessly, against the insidious incursion of placed products.

Straight (or 'spot') advertising suffers some significant disadvantages when compared to product placement. Advertisements do not always reach their target audience, and sometimes cannot do so – as in public sector broadcasting in the UK, which does not carry advertising. Television advertisements can be switched off, or fast forwarded, or programmed out. Alternatively, the viewer can simply leave the room while they are on. The audience may come to enjoy advertisements as a genre, singing the jingles and smiling at the jokes, without being influenced to make any purchases. Compared to straight advertising, product placement is thought to be a subtler, 'embedded' form of persuasion. It does not exhort us to buy, but works indirectly via viewer identification with characters or celebrities and their possessions. Characters and celebrities merge: both James Bond and Pierce Brosnan wear Omega watches. Product placement also lasts for as long as the film or programme is shown, enjoying an afterlife in television repeats and on video.

The aim of corporations and agencies acting on their behalf is that embedded products should be not merely present but integral to the action. A verbal reference is desirable, as in *Wall Street*: 'Get this kid a Molson Light.' Even better is when the product is handled in some way by a key character. A famous example cited by Murdock (1992: 227) is a scene from Steven Spielberg's 1982 motion picture, *ET*. The shy extraterrestrial creature is enticed from his hiding place by a trail of Reese's Pieces sweets. How could a censor edit this out while leaving the story intact?

The regulators' concern is that where product placement is permitted it should not influence the content of the material in which it is embedded. Arguably, though, this is a demand that cannot be met. It may be possible to prevent gross violations of editorial independence where corporations blatantly put pressure on writers, directors and producers. But pressure may not be needed. Anyone writing, directing or producing a commercial motion picture knows that some types of film are more likely to encourage product placement than others. A commercially minded producer does not need 'pressure' to come up with the right stuff.

Product placement is a force for conservatism. Corporations want to put their money into guaranteed box-office success, which means proven directors and celebrity stars. Consumers are seduced into identifying with celebrities, who are themselves identified with and constituted as commodities. Formulaic, predictable films are favoured, so that corporations have a clear idea of how their product will be presented. This is one reason why the James Bond movies are so popular with agencies placing products.

Murdock ends his analysis of product placement with observations on the intrusiveness of commercial discourse, which 'speaks to viewers as consumers and not as citizens' (1992: 228). Commodities are sold as the solution to personal problems, and social action is represented as no more than making the right purchase. This may explain why value-for-money consumerism has had so little impact on product placement. Paradoxically, this form of organized consumerism has been complicit with promotional culture.

The significance of consumer activism

Consumer organizations have received scant attention in the literature on consumption. They are represented in critiques of consumer society as part of the problem, not part of the solution. They depend upon and reinforce the principles of Fordist capitalism. Their efforts to supply consumers with information merely help the market to function efficiently. They are readily incorporated into the state's apparatus of legitimation, since they campaign on behalf of the mythical abstract 'consumer', not real citizens. Far from encouraging healthy abstention from consumption they tacitly promote indulgence in it, thereby reproducing the very seduction of consumers that they purport to oppose.

To commentators for whom consumer society is essentially a realm of self-expression, consumer organizations are at best banal and at worst irredeemably puritanical. Their goal is to strip consumption of all its symbolic and aesthetic connotations, so as to render it merely utilitarian. They treat consumers as incompetent victims and feeble dupes who need to have 'rationality' drummed into them. Consumer organizations may have a limited role in relieving the feelings of consumer guilt cultivated by self-dramatizing sections of the middle class: they may be consuming, but can console themselves that they are consuming rationally. Aside from this function, the mission of consumer organizations is not merely inconsequential but incoherent.

These two divergent critiques have one point in common: in denying the expressive aspect of consumption, and therefore ignoring the power of symbols, consumer organizations trivialize consumption.

There is, however, more to consumer activism than value-for-money consumer organizations. Their heyday has almost certainly passed, along with the Fordist era which gave them birth. The erosion of once solid foundations – career, community, social class, full employment, the welfare state, and the nation-state itself – implies that new forms of activism will emerge to engage with what Bauman (2000) calls the 'liquidity' and Urry (2000) the 'fluidity' of high modernity. Consumption has broken free from its former boundaries. Images, objects and people flow unstoppably across national frontiers, despite the border guards. For all its apparatus of repression, communism was unable to insulate itself against consumer capitalism. Markets are becoming global, and consumer activism is adapting to the trend. Naomi Klein's *No Logo* has attracted so much attention, and not only from the academic world, precisely because it examines the new modes of consumer action that are emerging to confront new configurations of power. The study of consumer activism is therefore crucial to our attempts to understand and engage with consumer society.

References

Aglietta, M. 1979: *A Theory of Capitalist Regulation: the US experience*. London: Verso.

Akerlof, G. A. 1970: The market for 'lemons': qualitative uncertainty and the market mechanism. *Quarterly Journal of Economics*, 84, 488–500.

Aldridge, A. 1994: The construction of rational consumption in *Which?* magazine: the more blobs the better? *Sociology*, 28 (4), 899–912.

Aldridge, A. 1997: Engaging with promotional culture: organized consumerism and the personal financial services industry. *Sociology*, 31 (3), 389–408.

Aldridge, A. 1998: *Habitus* and cultural capital in the field of personal finance. *Sociological Review*, 46 (1), 1–23.

Aldridge, A. 2000: *Religion in the Contemporary World: a sociological introduction*. Cambridge: Polity.

Aldridge, M. 1994: *Making Social Work News*. London and New York: Routledge.

Aldridge, M. 2001: The paradigm contingent career? Women in regional newspaper journalism. *Sociological Research Online*, 6 (3). ⟨http://www.socresonline.org.uk/6/3/aldridge.html⟩

Alexander, J. C. 1995. *Fin de Siècle Social Theory*. London and New York: Verso.

Arblaster, A. and Lukes, S. (eds) 1971: *The Good Society*. London: Methuen.

Barthes, R. 1972/1957: *Mythologies*. London: Cape.

Baudrillard, J. 1981: *For a Critique of the Political Economy of the Sign*. St Louis: Telos Press.

Baudrillard, J. 1983: *Simulations*. New York: Semiotext(e).
Bauman, Z. 1990: *Thinking Sociologically*. Oxford: Blackwell.
Bauman, Z. 1994: Desert spectacular. In K. Tester (ed.), *The Flâneur*. London: Routledge, 138–57.
Bauman, Z. 1998: *Work, Consumerism and the New Poor*. Buckingham: Open University Press.
Bauman, Z. 2000: *Liquid Modernity*. Cambridge: Polity.
Bauman, Z. 2001: Consuming life. *Journal of Consumer Culture*, 1 (1), 9–29.
Beardsworth, A. and Bryman, A. 1999: Late modernity and the dynamics of quasification: the case of the themed restaurant. *Sociological Review*, 47 (2), 228–57.
Beck, U. 1992: *Risk Society: towards a new modernity*. London: Sage.
Bell, D. 1979: *The Cultural Contradictions of Capitalism*, 2nd edn. London: Heinemann.
Bellah, R. N., Madsen, R., Sullivan, W. M., Swidler, A. and Tipton, S. M. 1996: *Habits of the Heart: individualism and commitment in American life*. Berkeley: University of California Press.
Bellamy, E. 1951/1888: *Looking Backward, 2000–1887*. New York: Random House.
Bender, C. and Poggi, G. 1999: Golden arches and iron cages: McDonaldization and the poverty of cultural pessimism at the end of the twentieth century. In B. Smart (ed.), *Resisting McDonaldization*, London: Sage, 22–40.
Benjamin, W. 1999: *The Arcades Project*. Cambridge, Mass.: Harvard University Press.
Berger, P. L. 1970: *A Rumour of Angels: modern society and the rediscovery of the supernatural*. Harmondsworth: Penguin.
Berlin, I. 1969: *Four Essays on Liberty*. Oxford: Clarendon Press.
Bocock, R. 1993: *Consumption*. London: Routledge.
Bourdieu, P. 1984: *Distinction: a social critique of the judgement of taste*. London: Routledge.
Bourdieu, P. et al. 1999: *The Weight of the World: social suffering in contemporary society*. Cambridge: Polity.
Bowlby, R. 2000: *Carried Away: the invention of modern shopping*. London: Faber.
Bryman, A. 1995: *Disney and his Worlds*. London: Routledge.
Bryman, A. 1999a: The Disneyization of society. *Sociological Review*, 47 (1), 24–47.
Bryman, A. 1999b: Theme parks and McDonaldization. In B. Smart (ed.), *Resisting McDonaldization*, London: Sage, 101–15.
Bryson, B. 1996: 'Anything but heavy metal': symbolic exclusion and musical dislikes. *American Sociological Review*, 61: 855–99.

Burgess, A. 2001: Flattering consumption: creating a Europe of the consumer. *Journal of Consumer Culture*, 1 (1), 93–117.

Burton, D. 1994: *Financial Services and the Consumer*. London and New York: Routledge.

Callinicos, A. 1999: *Social Theory: a historical introduction.* Cambridge: Polity.

Callinicos, A. 2001: *Against the Third Way: an anti-capitalist critique.* Cambridge: Polity.

Cameron, D. 2000: *Good to Talk? Living and working in a communication culture.* London: Sage.

Campbell, C. 1987: *The Romantic Ethic and the Spirit of Modern Consumerism.* Oxford: Blackwell.

Campbell, C. 1995: The sociology of consumption. In D. Miller (ed.), *Acknowledging Consumption: a review of new studies,* London: Routledge, 96–126.

Carey, J. (ed.) 1999: *The Faber Book of Utopias.* London: Faber.

Carrier, J. G. 1997: Introduction. In J. G. Carrier (ed.), *Meanings of the Market: the free market in western culture.* Oxford and New York: Berg, 1–67.

Carruthers, B. G. and Babb, S. L. 2000: *Economy/Society: markets, meanings and social structure.* Thousand Oaks: Pine Forge Press.

Casey, C. 1995: *Work, Self and Society: after industrialism.* London: Routledge.

Caute, D. 1988: *The Fellow-Travellers: intellectual friends of communism.* New Haven: Yale University Press.

Chaney, D. 1996: *Lifestyles.* London: Routledge.

Clammer, J. 1997: *Contemporary Urban Japan: a sociology of consumption.* Oxford: Blackwell.

Classen, C. and Howes, D. 1996: Epilogue: the dynamics and ethics of cross-cultural consumption. In D. Howes (ed.), *Cross-Cultural Consumption: global markets, local realities,* London and New York: Routledge, 178–94.

Coates, K. and Silburn, R. 1970: *Poverty: the forgotten Englishmen.* Harmondsworth: Penguin.

Corrigan, P. 1997: *The Sociology of Consumption: an introduction.* London: Sage.

Craib, I. 1989: *Psychoanalysis and Social Theory: the limits of sociology.* London: Harvester Wheatsheaf.

Dant, T. 1999: *Material Culture in the Social World: values, activities, lifestyles.* Buckingham: Open University Press.

Davis, J. 1992: *Exchange.* Buckingham: Open University Press.

de Botton, A. 1998: *How Proust can Change your Life.* London: Picador.

de Certeau, M. 1984: *The Practice of Everyday Life.* Berkeley: University of California Press.

Delanty, G. 1999: *Social Theory in a Changing World: conceptions of modernity.* Cambridge: Polity.

Douglas, M. 1973: *Natural Symbols: explorations in cosmology.* Harmondsworth: Penguin.

Douglas, M. and Isherwood, B. 1996: *The World of Goods: towards an anthropology of consumption.* London and New York: Routledge.

Drummond, G. 2001: Meet TV's newest stars. *The Guardian*, 23 July.

du Gay, P. 1996: *Consumption and Identity at Work.* London: Sage.

Eagleton, T. 1991: *Ideology: an introduction.* London: Verso.

Edwards, T. 2000: *Contradictions of Consumption: concepts, practices and politics in consumer society.* Buckingham: Open University Press.

Elliott, A. 2001: *Concepts of the Self.* Cambridge: Polity.

Eriksen, T. H. 1995: *Small Places, Large Issues: an introduction to social and cultural anthropology.* London: Pluto.

Etzioni, A. 1995: *The Spirit of Community: rights, responsibilities and the communitarian agenda.* London: Fontana.

Fairclough, N. 1994: Conversationalization of public discourse and the authority of the consumer. In R. Keat, N. Whiteley and N. Abercrombie (eds), *The Authority of the Consumer*, London and New York: Routledge, 253–68.

Featherstone, M. 1991: *Consumer Culture and Postmodernism.* London: Sage.

Ferguson, N. 2001: *The Cash Nexus: money and power in the modern world, 1700–2000.* London: Allen Lane.

Ferguson, P. P. 1994: The *flâneur* on and off the streets of Paris. In K. Tester (ed.), *The Flâneur*, London: Routledge, 22–42.

Finch, J. and Mason, J. 1993: *Negotiating Family Responsibilities.* London and New York: Tavistock/Routledge.

Finkelstein, J. 1989: *Dining Out: a sociology of modern manners.* Cambridge: Polity.

Fiske, J. 1989: *Understanding Popular Culture.* Boston: Unwin Hyman.

Fowles, J. 1996: *Advertising and Popular Culture.* London: Sage.

Frank, T. 2001: *One Market under God: extreme capitalism, market populism and the end of economic democracy.* London: Secker and Warburg.

Friedman, M. 1985: The changing language of a consumer society: brand name usage in popular American novels in the postwar era. *Journal of Consumer Research*, 11: 927–38.

Fukuyama, F. 1992: *The End of History and the Last Man.* Harmondsworth: Penguin.

Fukuyama, F. 1995: *Trust: the social virtues and the creation of prosperity*. London: Hamish Hamilton.

Fukuyama, F. 1999: *The Great Disruption: human nature and the reconstitution of social order*. London: Profile Books.

Gabriel, Y. 1999: *Organizations in Depth: the psychoanalysis of organizations*. London: Sage.

Gabriel, Y. and Lang, T. 1995: *The Unmanageable Consumer: contemporary consumption and its fragmentation*. London: Sage.

Galbraith, J. K. 1977: *The Age of Uncertainty*. London: Deutsch.

Gartman, D. 1994: *Auto Opium: a social history of American automobile design*. London and New York: Routledge.

Gendron, B. 1986: Theodor Adorno meets the Cadillacs. In T. Modleski (ed.), *Studies in Entertainment: critical approaches to mass culture*, Bloomington: Indiana University Press, 18–36.

Giddens, A. 1990: *The Consequences of Modernity*. Cambridge: Polity.

Giddens, A. 1991: *Modernity and Self-Identity: self and society in the late modern age*. Cambridge: Polity.

Goldthorpe, J. H., Lockwood, D., Bechhofer, F. and Platt, J. 1969: *The Affluent Worker in the Class Structure*. Cambridge: Cambridge University Press.

Gorz, A. 1999: *Reclaiming Work: beyond the wage-based society*. Cambridge: Polity.

Habermas, J. 1973: *Legitimation Crisis*. Boston: Beacon Press.

Hall, S. 1988: *The Hard Road to Renewal: Thatcherism and the crisis of the left*. London and New York: Verso.

Harvey, D. 1989: *The Condition of Postmodernity*. Oxford: Blackwell.

Heelas, P. 1991: Reforming the self: enterprise and the characters of Thatcherism. In R. Keat and N. Abercrombie (eds), *Enterprise Culture*, London: Routledge, 72–90.

Herbert, R. L. 1988: *Impressionism: art, leisure, and Parisian society*. New Haven and London: Yale University Press.

Hervieu-Léger, D. 2000: *Religion as a Chain of Memory*. New Brunswick: Rutgers University Press.

Hirschman, A. O. 1970: *Exit, Voice, and Loyalty: responses to decline in firms, organizations, and states*. Cambridge, Mass.: Harvard University Press.

Hochschild, A. R. 1983: *The Managed Heart: commercialization of human feeling*. Berkeley: University of California Press.

Hoggart, R. 1958: *The Uses of Literacy*. Harmondsworth: Penguin.

Horkheimer, M. and Adorno, T. W. 1973/1944: *Dialectic of Enlightenment*. London: Allen Lane.

Howes, D. 1996: Introduction: commodities and cultural borders. In D. Howes (ed.), *Cross-Cultural Consumption: global markets, local realities*, London and New York: Routledge, 1–16.

ITC (Independent Television Commission) 2001: *Programme Complaints and Findings, March 2001*. London: Independent Television Commission.

ITC (Independent Television Commission) 2002: *The ITC Programme Code*. London: Independent Television Commission.

James, N. 1989: Emotional labour: skills and work in the social regulation of feeling. *Sociological Review*, 37 (1), 15–42.

Jordan, B. 1999: Begging: the global context and international comparisons. In H. Dean (ed.), *Begging Questions: street-level economic activity and social policy failure*, Bristol: Policy Press, 43–62.

Kanter, R. M. 1993: *Men and Women of the Corporation*. New York: Basic Books.

Klein, N. 2000: *No Logo: taking aim at the brand bullies*. London: Flamingo.

Kumar, K. 1991: *Utopianism*. Buckingham: Open University Press.

Lasch, C. 1991/1977: *The Culture of Narcissism: American life in an age of diminishing expectations*. New York: Norton.

Lazar, D. 1990: *Markets and Ideology in the City of London*. London: Macmillan.

Lebergott, S. 1993: *Pursuing Happiness: American consumers in the twentieth century*. Princeton: Princeton University Press.

Lee, M. J. 1993: *Consumer Politics Reborn: the cultural politics of consumption*. London: Routledge.

Lewis, J. and Meredith, B. 1988: *Daughters Who Care*. London and New York: Routledge.

Liebowitz, S. J. and Margolis, S. E. 1990: The fable of the keys. *Journal of Law and Economics*, 22, 1–26.

Liebowitz, S. J. and Margolis, S. E. 1995: Path dependence, lock-in and history. *Journal of Law, Economics and Organization*, 11, 205–26.

Lipietz, A. 1987: *Mirages and Miracles: the crises of global Fordism*. London: Verso.

Lodziak, C. 2002: *The Myth of Consumerism*. London: Pluto Press.

López, J. 2003: *Society and its Metaphors: language, social theory and social structure*. London: Continuum Books.

Loudon, D. L. and Della Bitta, A. J. 1993: *Consumer Behavior: concepts and applications*. New York: McGraw-Hill.

Lukes, S. 1974: *Power: a radical view*. London: Macmillan.

Lury, C. 1996: *Consumer Culture*. Cambridge: Polity.

Lynd, R. S. and Lynd, H. M. 1937: *Middletown in Transition*. London: Constable.

Lyon, D. 1994: *Postmodernity*. Buckingham: Open University Press.

McGuigan, J. 1992: *Cultural Populism*. London: Routledge.

McIntosh, I. and Erskine, A. 1999: 'I feel rotten. I do, I feel rotten': exploring the begging encounter. In H. Dean (ed.), *Begging Questions: street-level economic activity and social policy failure*. Bristol: Policy Press, 183–202.

MacIntyre, A. 1985: *After Virtue*. London: Duckworth.

Marcuse, H. 1964: *One Dimensional Man: studies in the ideology of advanced industrial society*. London: Routledge and Kegan Paul.

Martin, B. 1981: *A Sociology of Contemporary Cultural Change*. Oxford: Blackwell.

Maslow, A. 1970: *Motivation and Personality*, 2nd edn. New York: Harper and Row.

Meyrowitz, J. 1985: *No Sense of Place: the impact of electronic media on social behaviour*. New York and Oxford: Oxford University Press.

Miles, S. 1998: *Consumerism as a Way of Life*. London: Sage.

Miles, S. 2000: *Youth Lifestyles in a Changing World*. Buckingham: Open University Press.

Miller, D. 1998: *A Theory of Shopping*. Cambridge: Polity.

Miller, D., Jackson, P., Thrift, N., Holbrook, B. and Rowlands, M. 1998: *Shopping, Place and Identity*. London: Routledge.

Minsky, R. 1998: *Psychoanalysis and Culture: contemporary states of mind*. Cambridge: Polity.

Morris, W. 1970/1890: *News from Nowhere, or, An Epoch of Rest*. London: Routledge.

Mort, F. 1989: The politics of consumption. In S. Hall and M. Jacques (eds), *New Times: the changing face of politics in the 1990s*, London: Lawrence and Wishart, 160–72.

Mouzelis, N. 1995: *Sociological Theory: What Went Wrong? Diagnosis and Remedies*. London and New York: Routledge.

Murdock, G. 1992: Embedded persuasions: the fall and rise of integrated advertising. In D. Strinati and S. Wagg (eds), *Come On Down? Popular media culture in post-war Britain*, London and New York: Routledge, 202–31.

Nader, R. 1991: *Unsafe at Any Speed: the designed-in dangers of the American automobile*. New York: Knightsbridge.

Norris, J. D. 1990: *Advertising and the Transformation of American Society, 1865–1920*. New York: Greenwood.

O'Neill, J. 1999: Have you had your theory today? In B. Smart (ed.), *Resisting McDonaldization*, London: Sage, 41–56.

O'Reilly, K. 2000: *The British on the Costa del Sol: transnational identities and local communities*. London and New York: Routledge.

Packard, V. 1957: *The Hidden Persuaders*. New York: Pocket Books.

Pahl, R. 1995: *After Success: fin-de-siècle anxiety and identity*. Cambridge: Polity.

Pahl, R. 2000: *On Friendship*. Cambridge: Polity.

Peters, T. J. and Waterman, R. H. 1982: *In Search of Excellence*. New York: Harper and Row.

Peterson, R. and Kern, R. 1996: Changing highbrow taste: from snob to omnivore. *American Sociological Review*, 61: 900–7.

Platt, J. 1971: *Social Research in Bethnal Green: an evaluation of the work of the Institute of Community Studies*. London: Macmillan.

Prendergrast, M. 1993: *For God, Country and Coca-Cola: the unauthorized history of the great American soft drink and the company that makes it*. Toronto: Maxwell Macmillan.

Putnam, R. D. 1995: Bowling alone: America's declining social capital. *Journal of Democracy*, 6 (1), 65–78.

Putnam, R. D. 2001: *Bowling Alone: the collapse and revival of American community*. London: Simon and Schuster.

Riesman, D. 1961: *The Lonely Crowd*: a reconsideration in 1960. In S. M. Lipset and D. Riesman (eds), *Culture and Social Character: the work of David Riesman reviewed*, New York: Free Press, 419–58.

Riesman, D. with Glazer, N. and Denney, R. 1961/1950: *The Lonely Crowd: a study of the changing American character*. New Haven: Yale University Press.

Ritzer, G. 1996: *The McDonaldization of Society: an investigation into the changing character of contemporary social life*. London: Sage.

Ritzer, G. 1997: *The McDonaldization Thesis: explorations and extensions*. London: Sage.

Ritzer, G. 1999a: Assessing the resistance. In B. Smart (ed.), *Resisting McDonaldization*, London: Sage, 234–55.

Ritzer, G. 1999b: *Enchanting a Disenchanted World: revolutionizing the means of consumption*, London: Sage.

Roche, M. 2000: *Mega-events and Modernity: Olympics, Expos and the growth of global culture*. London and New York: Routledge.

Rojek, C. 1993: *Way of Escape: modern transformations in leisure and travel*. London: Macmillan.

Rojek, C. and Turner, B. S. 2000: Decorative sociology: towards a critique of the cultural turn. *Sociological Review*, 48 (4), 629–48.

Sassatelli, R. 1995: Power balance in the consumption sphere: reconsidering consumer protection organizations. EUI Working Papers in Political and Social Sciences, no. 95/5, European University Institute, Florence.

Schumpeter, J. A. 1961: *Capitalism, Socialism and Democracy*. London: Allen and Unwin.

Scitovsky, T. 1976: *The Joyless Economy*. New York: Oxford University Press.

Scott, C. and Black, J. 2000: *Cranston's Consumers and the Law*, 3rd edn. London: Butterworths.

Scruton, R. 1998: Do the right thing. In P. 6 and I. Christie (eds), *The Good Life*, London: Demos, 49–54.

Sennett, R. 1998: *The Corrosion of Character: the personal consequences of work in the new capitalism*. New York: Norton.

Shields, R. 1994: Fancy footwork: Walter Benjamin's notes on *flânerie*. In K. Tester (ed.), *The Flâneur*, London: Routledge, 61–80.

Simmel, G. 1957/1904: Fashion. *American Journal of Sociology*, 62 (2), 541–58.

Simmel, G. 1971/1903: The metropolis and mental life. In D. Levine, *Georg Simmel: on individuality and social form*, Chicago: Chicago University Press.

Slater, D. 1997: *Consumer Culture and Modernity*. Cambridge: Polity.

Smith, A. 1970/1776: *The Wealth of Nations*. Harmondsworth: Penguin.

Smith, P. 1995: *Impressionism: beneath the surface*. London: Kalmann and King.

Stevenson, N. 2002: Consumer culture, ecology and the possibility of cosmopolitan citizenship. *Consumption, Markets and Culture*, forthcoming.

Storey, J. 1999: *Cultural Consumption and Everyday Life*. London: Arnold.

Strangleman, T. 2003: *Work Identity at the End of the Line? Privatization and culture change in the UK rail industry*. London: Sociology Press.

Strangleman, T. and Roberts, I. 1999: Looking through the window of opportunity: the cultural cleansing of workplace identity. *Sociology*, 33 (1), 47–67.

Strasser, S. 1989: *Satisfaction Guaranteed: the making of the American mass market*. Washington: Random House.

Strinati, D. 1995: *An Introduction to Theories of Popular Culture*. London and New York: Routledge.

Tester, K. 1999: The moral malaise of McDonaldization: the values of vegetarianism. In B. Smart (ed.), *Resisting McDonaldization*, London: Sage, 207–21.

Tomlinson, J. 1999: *Globalization and Culture*. Cambridge: Polity.

Urry, J. 2000: *Sociology beyond Societies: mobilities for the twenty-first century*. London and New York: Routledge.

Veblen, T. 1925/1899: *The Theory of the Leisure Class: an economic study of institutions*. London: Allen and Unwin.

Walker, R. and Collins, C. forthcoming: Families of the poor. In J. Treas et al. (eds), *Blackwell Companion on the Sociology of the Family*. Malden, Mass.: Blackwell.

Wallace, M. 1996: *Mickey Mouse History and Other Essays on American Memory*. Philadelphia: Temple University Press.

Warde, A. 2002: Setting the scene: changing conceptions of consumption. In S. Miles, A. Anderson and K. Meethan (eds), *The Changing Consumer: markets and meanings*, London and New York: Routledge, 10–24.

Warde, A. and Martens, L. 2000: *Eating Out: social differentiation, consumption and pleasure*, Cambridge: Cambridge University Press.

Warde, A., Martens, L. and Olsen, W. 1999: Consumption and the problem of variety: cultural omnivorousness, social distinction and dining out. *Sociology*, 33 (1), 105–27.

Wasko, J., Phillips, M. and Purdie, C. 1993: Hollywood meets Madison Avenue: the commercialization of US films. *Media, Culture and Society*, 15 (2), 271–93.

Weber, M. 1992/1904–5: *The Protestant Ethic and the Spirit of Capitalism*. London: Routledge.

Wernick, A. 1991: *Promotional Culture: advertising, ideology and symbolic expression*. London: Sage.

White, E. 2001: *The Flâneur: a stroll through the paradoxes of Paris*. London: Bloomsbury.

Whyte, William H. 1960: *The Organization Man*. Harmondsworth: Penguin.

Wilde, O. 1891: The soul of man under socialism. *Fortnightly Review*, 49.

Williams, R. 1973: *The Country and the City*. London: Chatto and Windus.

Williams, R. 1976: *Keywords: a vocabulary of culture and society*. Glasgow: Fontana.

Williamson, J. 1986: *Consuming Passions: the dynamics of popular culture*. London: Marion Boyars.

Young, M. and Willmott, P. 1962/1957: *Family and Kinship in East London*. Harmondsworth: Penguin.

Index

Lightning Source UK Ltd.
Milton Keynes UK
UKOW05f1202200314

9 780745 625300